BEHAVIOR
AND
EVOLUTION

Jean Piaget

BEHAVIOR
AND
EVOLUTION

Translated from the French by
Donald Nicholson-Smith

PANTHEON BOOKS
NEW YORK

LIBRARY OF CONGRESS CATALOGING IN PUBLICATION DATA

Piaget, Jean. 1896–
Behavior and Evolution.

Translation of *Le comportement moteur de l'évolution.*
Includes index.
1. Genetic psychology. 2. Movement, Psychology of.
I. Title.
BE702.P49313   1978   155.7   77-88762
ISBN 0-394-41810-7
ISBN 0-394-73588-9 pbk.

Manufactured in the United States of America

First American Edition

Contents

BEHAVIOR AND EVOLUTION

Translator's Acknowledgments

I would like to thank Dr. Gilbert Voyat for reading the translation, offering his criticisms and suggestions, and clearing up some difficulties in the text in consultation with Professor Piaget.

My thanks also to Ruth Elwell for her help in the preparation of the manuscript.

D. N.-S.

Introduction

By "BEHAVIOR" I refer to all action directed by organisms toward the outside world in order to change conditions therein or to change their own situation in relation to these surroundings. Examples would be searching for food, building a nest, using a tool, etc. At the lowest level, behavior amounts to no more than sensorimotor actions (perceptions and movements in conjunction); at the highest, it embraces ideational internalizations, as in human intelligence, where action extends into the sphere of mental operations. On the other hand, internal movements of the organism, such as the contraction of muscles or the circulation of blood, do not qualify as behavior in this sense, even though they condition behavior. Nor would we consider as behavior the action of respiration upon the atmosphere, because such action occurs as a result of processes not actually designed to affect the milieu. (The fact that it does indeed occur—and on a massive scale in the case of the oxygen produced by plants—is irrelevant for our purposes.) But an animal's reflexes, or the ornithogalum flower's reactions to light, may legitimately be described as behavior because they are intended, no matter how locally or occasionally, to modify the relationship between organism and environment. The same goes for perceptions, which are always a function of actual or virtual overall behavior. In sum, behavior is teleonomic action aimed at the utilization or transformation of the environment and the preservation or increase of the organism's capacity to affect this environment.

That there is a relationship between all forms of behavior so understood and the evolution of life in general is a widely accepted view. The nature of this relationship, however, is a question on which little consensus exists. Indeed, there are many possible ways of approaching the problem. Sometimes behavior is viewed as causal in relation to evolution, sometimes as determined by it. Sometimes a general solution is sought, and sometimes the interpretation varies according to the specific case, as when a distinction is drawn between forms of behavior associated with specialized organs and forms that seem to retain the quality of *acts*. The aim of this book is to present a critical examination of the different approaches to the problem of behavior. My concern, however, is not with behavior's internal mechanisms. That is a question for the ethologists. Rather, I want to evaluate behavior's role within the framework of the general processes of the evolution of life. This problem is rarely dealt with explicitly, as though its solution were implicit in any model of evolutionary diversity. But it may well be, to the contrary, that this role is fundamental as a necessary (though not sufficient) condition of evolution, and hence that the inability to account for this is adequate cause for rejecting a number of theories of organic and morpho-genetic changes, the classical status of these theories notwithstanding. Otherwise we shall run the risk of treat-ing intelligence itself, not to mention the science of biol-ogy, as a product of chance, and of failing to distinguish between the selection of accommodations on the basis of experience or of the surroundings and mere so-called natural selection, as gauged solely by survival and by the relative rate of reproduction. In the collective work *Be-havior and Evolution,*[1] G. G. Simpson maintains, admit-tedly, that the findings of modern ethology have made it impossible to consider behavior solely a result of evolu-tion and that it must also be treated as one of its determi-nants. But the central problem remains, for we still have to ascertain how behavior operates here, and whether it intervenes solely in selection and survival or also as a causal factor in the actual formation of morphological characteristics, as is suggested notably by Paul A. Weiss's conclusion that the living organism's overall organiza-tion and hierarchy of subsystems have a retroactive effect, according to the various forms of a "global dy-namics" (or "field" effects), even upon the functioning of the genome,[2] instead of being simply determined by this functioning.

In fact, all accounts of the role of behavior in evolu-
tional mechanisms have tended toward one or the other
of two extreme solutions. For the most part, it is only
very recently that any attempt has been made to develop
more subtle explanatory models. One of the two extreme positions is, of course, the Lamarckian one. This
approach treats changes in behavior, imposed by the
environment in the shape of types of new "habits," as the
source of all evolutionary variations, these then becoming fixed as heredity passes on the characteristics thus
acquired. Hence, Lamarckianism does look upon behavior as the central factor in evolution, although it also
postulates an internal factor known as organization. The
function of organization, however, is limited—to a
greater or lesser degree, depending on the text considered—to ensuring coordination between old and newly
acquired habits.

At the other extreme lies the orthodox neo-Darwinian
approach, which does not explicitly raise the question of
behavior's role but answers it implicitly by deeming any
new genotypical trait (including, therefore, any change
in hereditary behavior) to be the outcome of chance
variations whose adaptive nature emerges only after the
fact of natural selection,[3] with acquired characteristics
playing no part whatsoever. According to this account,
then, behavior has no active role in the generation of
evolutionary variations, and it comprises nothing more
than *effects* having no formative influence of any kind. It
is true that those types of behavior retained after selec-

tion are favorable to the survival of the species, but this is only by virtue of an *a posteriori* correlation between their fortuitous emergence and the requirements of the environment. The nature of this correlation is determined by no process other than the aggregation of chance developments. Generalizing from this position, Jacques Monod has gone even further than the neo-Darwinians, drawing the conclusion, on the basis of the chance factor which plays a part in all biological evolution, that such evolution is "not a property of living beings, since it stems from the very imperfections of the conservative mechanism which indeed constitutes their unique privilege."[4]

However, both these extreme positions, the motives for whose adoption I shall discuss below, are indicative of just how complex the problem of behavior's role in evolution becomes once we assume that it does indeed have a formative function and is not merely the outcome of hereditary morphological variations generated quite independently of the living organism that is to make use of them in its specific surroundings. Actually, new forms of behavior are often produced only in the course of an organism's development, or even in its maturity, and only where certain environmental conditions are fulfilled. In such cases, it would seem that the form of behavior in question is linked with epigenesis (during which interaction between genetic programming and environmental factors is already operative) or with a phenotypical state. This difficulty does not arise if one adopts the Lamarckian view that phenotypical variations are transmitted by heredity, and this is what enables Lamarck to consider changes in habits the basic factor in evolutionary transformations. At the other extreme, those who not only reject the possibility of such direct transmission in view of experimental findings that refute it, but also (and this is quite a different matter) treat genic mechanisms as radically independent of and alien to the retroactive effects of epigenesis, must view behavior as brought into being by the organism's genetic structures—by structures, in other words, created quite independently of behavior itself. In this case, it becomes extremely hard to explain how behavior can achieve such differentiated and sophisticated adaptations to an outside world that governs it solely by means of selective rejection or acceptance.

Thus, it is easy to see why those biologists who are not prepared to overlook either behavior's important formative role or the complexity of epigenesis cannot espouse either of the two extreme theses and why they seek more refined solutions. As early as 1896—i.e., before the revival of Mendelism and the neo-Darwinism that developed out of it—the great psychologist J. M. Baldwin[5] brought forward the very important notion of an "organic selection" based on the actual activity of the living organism as it seeks to "accommodate" to new surroundings the hereditary equipment with which it has been endowed. According to Baldwin, such accommodations, though not inherited directly, influence heredity and evolution and indirectly determine their course, thus orienting subsequent genetic variations in a fashion analogous to the working of "natural" selection.[6] Thus, Hovasse, using modern terminology, is able to define the "Baldwin effect" quite simply as "the possibility of an accommodation's being replaced by a mutation." This amounts to equating the "Baldwin effect" with C. H. Waddington's "genetic assimilation." But the interesting point for our purposes is that by eking out the selection accomplished by the environment with his "organic selection," Baldwin opened the door to the idea of the organism itself affecting the inception and canalization of new hereditary forms, and this as a consequence of its exploratory behavior.

Waddington also adopts a middle-of-the-road position when he asserts that natural selection can only affect phenotypes, with all the interactions that their epigenesis entails between hereditary syntheses and environmental influences. Thus, he does not hesitate to break the taboo on talking in terms of "inheritance of acquired characteristics." But instead of conceiving of this in Lamarckian fashion as resulting from the direct influence of the environment, he introduces a mechanism of internal and external selection which he calls genetic assimilation. The important point for us here is that Waddington does not look upon these processes of selection as something passively undergone by the organism. In his view, the organism in effect "chooses its environment"; behavior is a determinant of selection as much as a result of it, in accordance with one of the basic feedback systems described by this great biological pioneer. In his latest work, Waddington reinforces instances of genetic assimilation studied in the laboratory by citing my example of the pond snail *Limnaea stagnalis* as a verifiable instance occurring in nature[7]: I found that in parts of the great Swiss lakes where *Limnaea* is exposed to intense wave action, contracted phenotypes produced by the animal's movements during growth are coupled with genotypes characterized by the same contraction, now capable of hereditary transmission (var. *L. lacustris* and *L. bodamica*).

A third author to whose work I shall be referring at length is Paul A. Weiss, one the most independent-minded and original biologists of the present time. Weiss has been bold enough, for example, to ask what, if anything, "the dramatic progress made in molecular genetics and, on a minor scale, developmental genetics" have taught us about "developmental *organization.*" And he concludes: "To this question an honest and informed answer can only be an unqualified 'nothing.' "[8] Hence, Weiss's very valuable piece of advice: "Let us then turn from more or less figmental notions as being the monopolistic sources of developmental order."[9] As for behavior, Weiss has devoted to the subject a book in which he stresses the fact that behavior is constituted by "systemic reactions." The systems in question are those overall organizations of which it can be said that variations in the whole are less than the sum of the variations in the component elements, and that this whole influences the subsystems (including genomes) by means of the global dynamics to which we have already referred.[10] There is no need to emphasize the capital importance which this approach must have in any discussion of the problem with which we are concerned, that of the relationship between behavior and the processes that shape evolution.

We shall also be led in this connection to consider the relationship between behavior and the mechanisms of phenocopy,[11] as described by a variety of authors. For, clearly, where a phenotypical variation precedes the constitution of the genotype, it becomes possible, during this first stage, to directly evaluate the eventual role of behavioral changes. On the other hand, it is equally clear that such cases, although they offer a privileged vantage point for our purposes, cannot be made the basis for a generalization covering all situations that involve hereditary behavior; in this area the great mystery remains the formation of complex and specialized instincts, for to attribute a phenotypical origin to such instincts would result in our assigning very superior intelligence to relatively inferior animals. Therefore, we have to pay close attention to the positions taken on these questions by the various ethological schools; for no matter how obscure the issue remains, in the last reckoning all knowledge of the relationship between behavior and the mechanism of the evolution of life in general depends on our conception of the nature of instincts. (Chapter Seven is devoted to a discussion of this problem.)

The question I want to raise and deal with here, like all questions concerning the establishment of relationships, is at once central and hard to demarcate. I do not propose another discussion of the various theories of evolution, nor is it my aim to justify some *via media* between Lamarckianism and neo-Darwinism,[12] after the fashion of so many well-intentioned people today. Even further from my intent is the exposition of the various conceptions of behavior, this being the task of the presently flourishing discipline known as ethology. The goal I have set myself is at first sight a much simpler one: the examination and discussion of the different possible hypotheses regarding the role of behavior in the mechanisms of evolution. This is complicated, however, by the fact that behavior on the one hand and evolutionary mechanisms on the other are accounted for in terms of many and very diverse explanatory models. Consequently, I have no choice but to refer to these different senses of the two factors whose relationship I wish to determine. More importantly, the very choice of this problem naturally implies a certain ambition on my part. There is, after all, no point in seeking to establish the nature of a relationship unless this throws light upon the facts or concepts whose links are at issue.

In the case of the relationship between behavior and biological evolution, it would indeed seem that the better our acquaintanceship with it, the clearer must our understanding of evolutionary mechanisms become. And this for a reason which is basic, although it is often forgotten: it is behavior which calls forth that diversity (and, ultimately, specificity) in forms of adaptation for which the evolution of life is necessarily responsible; for behavior, be it cause or effect, is inextricably bound up with the life of the organism.

The central problem of biology is, in fact, the coordination between endogenous evolutionary changes and the multiform exogenous action of environment, an action that requires adaptations of various kinds. Once it is granted that the environment does not act directly upon the genome, the simplest solution is obviously to explain adaptation by selection. If selection is presumed to preserve the fittest, however, this aptitude can only be gauged by the degree of survival,[13] the sole yardstick of selection itself, whence the equation: adaptation = survival. But while it is true that the adaptations that characterize varieties of behavior all naturally facilitate survival, they also have a much broader raison d'être in that they serve to increase the powers of the individual or species by putting greater means at their disposal—means which require that behavior be adapted to often highly differentiated aspects of the environment. Such adaptations embody a "savoir-faire" presupposing a work of accommodation on the part of the organism itself, and not merely an automatic sorting procedure effected from without on the basis of what does or does not foster survival. We are forced to conclude that the ultimate aim of behavior is nothing less than the expansion of the habitable—and, later, of the knowable—environment. This expansion begins as "exploration" in animals of various degrees of complexity, but it extends far beyond the needs of immediate utility, and of precautions, until we find it operating on levels where a part is played by simple curiosity about objects or events, as well as by the subject's pursuit of every possible activity. There exists, therefore, a practical and cognitive adaptation far more general in nature than adaptation-survival, an adaptation that calls not only for selection's mechanisms of accept-ance and rejection but also for a structuring of the envi-ronment by the organism itself.

Thus, the consideration of behavior must necessarily alter models of evolution that work well enough when this factor is (unjustifiably) ignored. As long as one is concerned solely with morphological variations at the level of the mutation, there may be a case for working with the hypothesis of random endogenous mutations and an exogenous selection process that merely deter-mines which of these should be retained and which elimi-nated. But to the extent that the new variation must meet the requirements of a given specialized characteristic of the environment, as is true in varying degrees for all practical and cognitive adaptations, the need for an ac-count of the links between formative endogenous factors and exogenous actions becomes ever more pressing. Meeting this need is indeed the goal of those contempo-rary theories that seek to transcend neo-Darwinism without simply reverting to Lamarckianism. The point is that there is a basic difference between the hereditary mechanism which ensures the transmission of a particular form (morphogenesis) and that which transmits a type of behavior. The epigenetic development of a simple form progresses through continuous biochemical reactions from the genome to the final form. This final form is the end point of a succession of syntheses determined by the genome, the structural point of origin. Types of behavior, by contrast, also call into play a number of actions, of movements, which go beyond the bounds of the organism and which, because they are brought to bear upon the outside world, cannot be *preformed* in the genome, even if they are in some sense *programmed* by it. In what sense, though? How can movements be programmed if they have never been executed, and if they are not modeled on movements employed previously? A type of behavior cannot be the result of biochemical reactions until these reactions are themselves oriented toward a result sought as a goal. So, whereas the first phases of morphogenesis involve only internal organization with its immanent teleonomy, behavior, even in its most primitive form, implies a different kind of orientation, different goals transcending the somatic framework and signaling the beginning of a necessary opening-up onto the universe. It is this exchange with the environment which gives rise to the specific problems of a genetic account of behavior, as distinct from the problem of morphology in general. The explanation of hereditary behavior, and

specifically of the formation of such behavior, requires
that the relationship between endogenous and exogenous factors be constantly borne in mind. The aim of the
present work is an exposition and discussion of the solutions which have been offered, or which might well be
offered, to this cardinal problem.

The neo-Darwinians see no need in this connection for
a distinction between variations occurring in the morphological structure of one type of tissue—that of the liver,
for example—and such variations occurring in tissue of
another type, such as that of the brain. Thus, they perceive no qualitative difference between the evolution of
anatomical structures and the evolution of "behavioral"
structures. At most, they accept that the innate factors in
the construction of superior forms of behavior (notably
"intelligence" in man) are merely a group of possibilities
consonant with the particular "genetic envelope" involved. In the case of instinctive behavior, where the role
of innate factors is much greater, we have, if we are going
to explain adaptation in terms of "adequation" or of
savoir-faire and no longer solely in terms of survival, to
postulate the existence of a comparable, though much
more primitive mechanism, quite material in character,
naturally, yet with sufficient heuristic value to account for
the formation of variations as such. Just as morphological
variation is ultimately the outcome of a recombination of
characteristics that have already been selected as
adapted, so behavioral variation may be supposed to take
as its starting point certain "elementary" variations which

already supply information about the environment. (This question is discussed in Chapter Four and Chapter Seven.) But these basic variations have then to be synthesized—not through a simple process of recombination resulting from chance conjunction but rather thanks to internal and inducible combinations capable of generating new possible adaptations (see Chapter Six). In other words, morphological variations eventually lead to adaptations, but to adaptations that can only be evaluated after the fact (i.e., in the light of the results of the selection-survival process). Behavioral variations, on the other hand, apparently tend toward greater and greater complexity—they tend in a direction which, although a detailed prefigurement of relationships with the environment can naturally never be achieved, does lead to the establishment of a more or less broad range of actualizable adequations. But it is important to note—and I shall have occasion to stress the fact—that this account does not imply the subordination of instincts to an intelligence operative from the outset. It merely draws logical conclusions about the self-regulatory functions that link the genome to epigenetic levels at which epigenesis is susceptible to modification by the action of the environment—hence the possibility of a "genetic assimilation" or of a phenocopy of learned behavior, and of a combinatory system permitting the composition of new, more complex forms of behavior, though at first in the shape of virtual coordinations which may or may not be actualized, depending on the circumstances.

Notes to Introduction

1. A. Rowe and G. G. Simpson, eds., *Behavior and Evolution* (New Haven: Yale University Press, 1958).

2. "Genome" refers to the total chromosomic apparatus, including its hereditary features.

3. It should be pointed out that chance factors come into play on two different levels in the neo-Darwinian doctrine. On the first level, mutations supply new, fortuitous variations. These are subjected to an initial process of selection, retaining only those among them which are adapted. In the course of secondary processes, the Mendelian segregation of chromosomes leads, in the case of sexual reproduction, to a recombination of parts (crossing over). This recombination, itself fortuitous but now affecting only those traits preserved on account of their adaptedness, is in turn subjected to selection. Seen from this angle, therefore, the conservative mechanism of reproduction does not exclude variation. It even makes it inevitable, for reasons analogous to those which operate in thermodynamic interaction. But it should be understood that all innovation is nevertheless seen as an outcome of chance, the two successive processes of selection being the sole cause of the exclusive conservation of favorable variations.

4. Jacques Monod, *Le hasard et la nécessité, essai sur la philosophie naturelle de la biologie moderne* (Paris: Seuil, 1970), p. 130. English trans.: *Chance and Necessity: An Essay on the Natural Philosophy of Modern Biology* (New York: Knopf, 1971), p. 116.

5. A figure largely forgotten by the psychologists, but more

and more frequently cited, in connection with the "Baldwin effect," by biologists, who are, however, unaware of his psychological work.

6. See J. M. Baldwin, *Mental Development in the Child and the Race* (1894). Reprint of third revised edition of 1906 (New York: Augustus M. Kelly, 1968).

7. See C. H. Waddington, *The Evolution of an Evolutionist* (Ithaca, New York: Cornell University Press, 1975), Chap. 9. As a matter of fact, I am no longer certain that "genetic assimilation" is the only factor involved here.

8. "The Basic Concept of Hierarchic Systems." In Paul A. Weiss *et al., Hierarchically Organized Systems in Theory and Practice* (New York: Hafner, 1971), p. 34.

9. Ibid, p. 39.

10. See especially ibid., Fig. 5, p. 40, where Weiss schematizes the feedback systems of the entire organism right down to the genic level.

11. "Phenocopy" refers to a biological process in which "an exogenous phenotype is neither interiorized nor fixed, but followed by and entirely replaced by a genotype of the same form, now reconstructed by purely endogenous mechanisms." (Jean Piaget, "From Noise to Order: The Psychological Development of Knowledge and Phenocopy in Biology," *Urban Review* no. 3 [1975]: 8, 209.)

12. See Jean Piaget, *Biology and Knowledge: An Essay on the Relations Between Organic Regulations and Cognitive Processes* (Chicago: Chicago University Press, 1971).

13. The reader should bear in mind that when I speak here and in what follows of "survival," I am merely employing a convenient shorthand. The survival in question is that of the species as a whole, not of particular individuals, and so the term covers all the factors determining the "differential rate of reproduction." For multiplication does not depend solely on relative survival; it may even be quite independent of it, as in

cases where rates of reproduction are governed by the number of offspring. These connotations should be taken as read wherever the blanket term "survival" is used in a conventional way for the sake of convenience.

BEHAVIOR AND EVOLUTION

ONE

———————

The Merits and Drawbacks of the Lamarckian Thesis

LAMARCK'S IDEAS concerning the role of behavior are of great interest on two counts. In the first place, Lamarck is undoubtedly the author who most clearly recognized behavior's importance for the morphogenesis of particular organs. Secondly, however, he limited this importance for two reasons which deserve close examination because between them there may be an unclarified relationship which will be very instructive for our purposes. The first reason is that Lamarck assigns an essentially exogenous origin to behavior ("actions" or "habits"), which he sees as determined by the "circumstances" peculiar to the various environments inhabited by organisms, overlooking the fact that all behavior implies the intervention of endogenous factors. The second reason is that for Lamarck the "habits" engendered by such environmental pressures, while certainly giving rise to a multiplicity of variations, do so within the framework of a process of global organization that constitutes the internal motor of evolution and is the outcome of neither behavior nor the environment. If we compare the various passages in Lamarck's work where he seeks to demarcate the frontier between "the power progressively to constitute organization" and "subjection to the influences of circumstances," we are inevitably struck by how difficult he seems to find this task, and even by contradictions, which he is hard put to dispose of, between the different accounts he offers according to which of these two aspects of evolution he happens to be stressing. So it may be helpful to ask why Lamarck did not link these two questions together; for to have given full weight, within behavior itself, to endogenous components would have made behavior quite compatible with the laws of organization, and, inversely, to have made organization part and parcel of the activity of living things would have effectively broadened this notion. What assumptions prevented Lamarck from formulating a unified approach of this kind, after the fashion now so familiar to us thanks to the modern concept of self-regulation?

1. First let us consider Lamarck's conception of behavior as formative of morphological variations. His thesis would appear to be quite unambiguous: "These actions and habits depend entirely on the circumstances in which we usually find ourselves," he asserts right from the outset of his discussion of the question in chapter 7 of *Philosophie zoologique*. Admittedly, he points out soon thereafter that between "circumstances" and the "habits" they engender, an intermediary role is played by "needs." He thus gives the impression that he is appealing to endogenous factors, but this is misleading because he immediately announces that "if new needs become constant or very long lasting, the animal will develop

4

new habits." Such changes in needs are themselves due to "changes in circumstances." Hence Lamarck's central interpretation (already formulated in his *Recherches sur les corps vivants*): "It is not an animal's organs—that is, the nature and form of the parts of its body—which have given rise to its habits and peculiar faculties; on the contrary it is its habits, its mode of life, and the circumstances in which its forebears came together, which, over time, have generated the form of its body, the number and condition of its organs and, in sum, the faculties with which it is endowed." The instances cited in support of this view are legion, and, without returning to the vexed question of the giraffe, it is worth mentioning the discussions of the webbed feet of frogs, turtles, otters, beavers, and other palmipeds, so clearly distinct from the hooked claws of tree-dwelling birds or from the long feet and long necks of waders.

But even though it is to Lamarck's great credit that he raised the problem, still pertinent today, of the relationship between the constitution of specialized organs and that of types of behavior, his account lacks any discussion of a preliminary question. Where the surroundings have not changed on the spot (which is unusual), what causes an animal or plant population to move to another environment without being obliged to do so by an increase in the pressure of competition (which is also unusual)? A solution often put forward today (by Waddington and others) is that the organism can "choose" its environment. Even Monod, whose position on the "chance" and non-necessity involved in evolution is well known, notes accurately that we owe the existence of vertebrate quadrupeds to the fact that "a primitive fish 'chose' to do some exploring on land, where its only means of locomotion was flapping."[1] Here are three examples which I myself have studied closely. First, the Alpine environment of the canton of Valais is inhabited by a small mollusk of the *Vitrina* family *(V. nivalis).* This snail lives between the altitudes of 2,500 and 3,000 meters, in surroundings that are extremely uncomfortable for it, especially since its shell is very thin, fragile, and translucent. *Vitrina* may also be found between sea level and the 2,500-meter mark, though not in any great abundance, so there can be no question of treating the choice of habitat of the high-altitude varieties as a response to competition or overcrowding. My second example is that of *Limnaea stagnalis,* which I have already mentioned. The species normally inhabits placid marshes and waters, but the variety *L. lacustris* has "chosen" beaches and rocky areas where the water is often agitated by wave action, although it might as easily have restricted itself to sheltered coves or gone down to a depth of ten to thirty meters, as did one sublittoral variety of the same species (which I have called var. *Bollingeri*). Third, we have the case of *Xerophila obvia,* an Eastern European snail carried westward in grass seed. In 1911 I came across a small colony of these snails established in the Valais at a low altitude. A few years later they had spread almost throughout the canton, on some mountains reaching altitudes radically different from those to which they had been accustomed.

In these three cases, typical of hundreds of others, it seems clear that new habits have not been imposed by changes in the environment occurring independently of the animal. Rather, the organism has conquered its new environment through an activity that has certainly also had a part to play in accommodations to the circumstances. Such accommodations are of course necessitated by this new environment, but only conditionally, not imperatively, for nothing obliged the conquering populations to adopt these surroundings rather than avoid them.

2. Thus, we find ourselves confronted right away by a general problem that will be coming up constantly: the problem of the teleonomy and orientation of behavior. — The first point to be noted is that while the formation of a new habit implies an "accommodation" to external situations—to put it in Baldwinian terms—this accommodation is always based on an earlier behavior pattern. In the last fifty years, the gulls of French Switzerland have taken to feeding on worms in the fields, flocking for this purpose behind the motorized plows that turn the worms up in great numbers. This habit was unknown formerly, when the gulls never left the lakes. But it is clear that such accommodation is founded on pre-existing patterns—patterns, in this case, of food-seeking. Therefore, we may say that in all animal behavior, including all behavior observed in children and in humans in general, any accommodation is linked to a process of practical or cognitive assimilation, where this is understood as an integration into a pre-existing behavioral structure (whether we are dealing with a savoir-faire, a conceptual schema, etc.). The fact that assimilation plays a part in every instance constitutes an initial argument— and a decisive one in itself—in favor of the necessity of endogenous factors or processes in all behavior.

If this is granted, it follows naturally that the first goal or orientation of behavior must be the fueling of patterns of assimilation or, in other words, the continuous or periodic exercise of already constituted patterns of action, making use of elements supplied by the environment. What we are envisaging here is a sort of practical metabolism, a metabolic system functioning at the practical or cognitive level. Every system of action or knowledge presupposes an internal organization of patterns that can only function when fueled by a group of external elements—hence the permanence of interaction between action and environment.

From the fact that every pattern of action—and thus of assimilation as just defined—allows for a greater or lesser number of possibilities of accommodation (according to its "reaction norm," to borrow a well-known biological term), it follows that such a pattern's maintenance, unlike that of physiological (chemical or energetic) assimilation, does not call for stability. On the contrary, it can only tend to be reinforced as long as survival is not threatened. Behavior is not centered on survival. Far from it, it tends to broaden its specific field of action through the independent reinforcement of patterns. And this, to my mind, is behavior's most important defining characteristic: a gradual expansion of the environment and, concomitant with it, an increase in the organism's capacity to affect this expanding environment. This is what makes possible the phenomena just reviewed, phenomena which can be described in terms of "choices" but which, to be more accurate, consist in successive conquests due to the enlargement of the field of application of existing patterns.

• • •

3. If such an endogenous behavioral dynamic does indeed exist, Lamarck's dualism between organizational factors and determination by outside circumstances becomes susceptible of a synthetic resolution which Lamarck himself, whose formulations remained in many ways contradictory, was unable to effect.

At times Lamarck presents the two sorts of causes as distinct in kind and even as working at odds: ". . . the state in which we find animals is the product, on the one hand, of the growing complexity of organization which tends to form an ordered gradation, and, on the other hand, of the influences exerted by a multitude of very diverse circumstances, influences which are constantly working to break down the regularity of gradation in the growing complexity of organization."[2] Alternatively, he contrasts organization, seen as "nature's plan," with "an extraneous cause" which "interferes here and there with the execution of this plan."

On the other hand, as soon as he returns to the question of environmental influences and of the formation of habits, which seems to be his preferred terrain, Lamarck ends up admitting the idea that circumstances have an effect on organization as such, in that "by becoming quite different they eventually change both the form and organization itself."[3] We have already seen how, in Lamarck's view, behavior modifies the organs or "parts" of the animal, and he adds that behavior "can even generate organs that did not formerly exist." He goes so far as to treat the animal's repeated actions—explained causally in terms of "influxes" of nervous "fluids"—as "acts of organization" (!) which "develop and even cre-

9

ate the organs they require."[4] But, most importantly, at the end of this same chapter 7 of *Philosophie zoologique,* Lamarck evokes two possible conclusions. The first, in which "almost everyone concurs," is the fact of organization itself. The second—"strictly my own"—is that circumstances act upon habits, and habits "upon the state of the parts and even upon organization." Hence the following massive assertion: "If I intended to pass in review all the classes, orders, genera and species of existing animals, I should be able to show that the conformation and structure of individuals, their organs, faculties, etc., are everywhere a pure result of the environment to which each species is exposed . . ."

Therefore, it does not seem excessive to infer, as I did in *Biology and Knowledge,*[5] that, in the light of his interpretation of habits as exclusively due to external circumstances, what Lamarck calls the "growing complexity of organization" is to be understood after the fashion of associationism and tends to be indistinguishable from the coordination of habits themselves in an overall system analogous to what Hull, in psychology, has since referred to as "families of habits." Sometimes (and sporadically, depending on the text considered), Lamarck tends to conceive of habits as "acts of organization" and is thus inclined to treat organization as the "complexity" *(composition)* of habits themselves. And sometimes he simply lets both kinds of causes stand, leaving a self-contradictory account in which no synthesis is attempted.

4. These difficulties stem entirely from Lamarck's empiricist interpretation of behavior. This he sees as exclusively determined by the environment, and he assigns no part to endogenous factors of the same order as organizational ones. But if, instead, we treat behavior as an extension of organization, though specialized in the sphere of functional (as opposed to material or energetic) exchanges between organism and environment, then syntheses will become possible. Such syntheses will involve us, of course, in the most far-reaching problems, because we shall still have to coordinate hereditary variations with the action of the environment, and this without evoking the direct inheritance of acquired characteristics postulated by the Lamarckians. But by identifying the group of mechanisms common, on the one hand, to the various forms of organization of living things (i.e., genetic, epigenetic, morphological, and physiological) and, on the other hand, to the forms of behavior, it should be possible to clarify the relationship between behavior and the evolution of life in general without returning to the fruitless discussion in which Lamarck became embroiled because he had no adequate interpretation of what he mistakenly lumped together under the rubric of habits: both inherited instincts and habits in the strict sense, which he treated as phenotypical because he assumed that the former were merely an extension of the latter.

This is not the place to deal generally with these common mechanisms, since we are concerned for the moment only with Lamarckianism. Yet a few remarks are in order, even within the limited context of Lamarck's great contribution, which remains so stimulating by virtue of its ambitions. A first point has to do with the prime characteristic attributed by Lamarck to "organization." He sees this as the outcome of a "growing complexity" and as manifesting a "regular gradation," whereas "circumstances" and the "habits" that these impose are seen merely as disturbing influences upon it. This notion of "gradation," close attention to which has so rarely been paid since Lamarck's time, has reappeared in contemporary biology in the work of Julian Huxley and Rensch, who seek to invest the concept of "progress" with an objective meaning. Huxley proposes two criteria, a "growing independence" of the organism vis-à-vis the surroundings and, in conjunction with this, an increasingly efficient "control" of the environment by the organism. For his part, Rensch evokes a gradual "opening up" consisting in an increase in the possibilities or capacities acquired by living things. In this context, it is clear that while these traits are transmitted morphologically and physiologically by means of a twofold process of correlated and progressive differentiation and integration, they nevertheless remain closely bound up with behavior itself. Independence in regard to the external environment does not depend solely on the stability of the internal environment (as Claude Bernard realized) but also on the animal's mobility; control of the surroundings is naturally partly a function of the action exerted on the environment by the organism, and hence of behavior. As for Rensch's gradual opening-up process, it goes without saying that this is brought about in large part thanks to new forms of behavior. When progress is envisaged in this way, it seems clear that progress in forms of behavior and progress in organization are one and the same thing, and this contrasts sharply with the Lamarckian view, according to which behavior tends to work counter to gradation. For here external circumstances are constantly being exploited, modified, and on occasion even provoked, by an active organism, instead of being simply imposed from without as they are in the empiricist view.

Let us now return to the question of the extending of the environment, which from what we have said seems to be the most general aim of behavior, always bearing in mind that this is correlated with the growth of capacities (Lamarck's "faculties"). I gave some account of this in chapter 22 of *Biology and Knowledge.* Every organism constitutes an open system in Bertalanffy's sense; its self-conservation depends on constant exchange with the environment in respect to the needs for nutrition and for protection against predators. Any such system is permanently threatened by its limitations and, even where the environment of the moment can meet immediate needs, the development of the most primitive precautionary and anticipatory behavior will eventually expand it. There is a tendency for the "organism-environment" system to become closed, a tendency which, needless to say, must constantly be countered—hence the pressure for the gradual expansion of the environment. But the environment is extended as a knowable if not immediately utilizable one. And the environment's knowable aspect is the proper domain of behavior, not of existing forms of physiological exchange.

This process, which may be identified in animals whose organization is of the most primitive kind, is naturally reinforced as soon as simple precautionary behavior gives way to the curiosity of the higher vertebrates, and even more so when actions become susceptible of ideational internalization and the door is opened to the indefinite expansion of the need for knowledge characteristic of human thought. Yet within the different kinds of behavior a distinction still has to be drawn between phenotypical activities and inherited instinctual forms, and this is a problem that Lamarckianism does not raise —or, rather, one which it "resolves" by assuming a basic continuity between the two. In fact, the relationship between these two kinds of behavior raises the most difficult question with which we shall have to deal as we approach the general problem of behavior's role in the evolutionary process itself.

Notes to Chapter One

1. Jacques Monod, *Le hasard et la nécessité* (Paris: Seuil, 1970), p. 142. Trans.: *Chance and Necessity* (New York: Knopf, 1971), p. 126.

2. *Philosophie zoologique,* 2 vols. (Paris, 1809, 1830). English trans. by Hugh Eliot: *Zoological Philosophy,* London, 1914; New York: Hafner, 1963. See chapter 7.

3. Ibid.

4. Ibid.

5. Jean Piaget, *Biology and Knowledge: An Essay on the Relations Between Organic Regulations and Cognitive Processes* (Chicago: Chicago University Press, 1971).

TWO

Baldwin and Organic Selection

TWO CONTRIBUTIONS marked the decisive turning point in evolutionary theory in the latter half of the nineteenth century: Darwin's explanation of evolution in terms of natural selection and Weissmann's rejection of the thesis of inherited acquired traits. Actually, however, the Darwinian solution does not in any way reduce the importance of environmental factors; it merely replaces the direct causal effects in which Lamarck believed with a probabilistic and statistical effect based on chance conjunctions between variations in the organism and external conditions, and on a selection process producing adequate adaptations. As for variations themselves, Darwin again offers a probabilistic account; they are said to be a function of the size and density of populations and of the accumulation of successive generations, all these being causes of congenital fluctuations or variations. The essential difference from Lamarckianism here is that Darwin assigns virtually no role to ontogenesis or to individual forms of behavior, with the exception of the sexual instincts. This was precisely what psychologist J.

M. Baldwin found troublesome in the Darwinian theory and the reason why, in his well-known article "A New Factor in Evolution," published in 1896 in the *American Naturalist,* and in his book *Mental Development in the Child and the Race* (1894), he sought to round out Darwinism, though not to refute it, by introducing the notion of "functional selection" or, more specifically, "organic selection."

1. Baldwin's starting point is "natural" selection in Darwin's sense of the term: "On our theory, the first adaptation is *phylogenetic;* i.e., it is a variation. By the operation of natural selection among organisms, those survive which respond by expansion to certain stimulations of food, oxygen, etc., and by contraction to other certain stimulations . . ."[1] Positive responses of this kind still have to be explained, however, and here Baldwin evokes reactions of "excess" and "reinforcements" (also called over-production), which we should now refer to as positive feedback systems; and he attributes this "learning of new movements"[2] to a process of "functional selection," which already requires an activity on the part of the organism itself.

But, more than this, the organism is also capable of bringing about variations in its congenital traits or capacities by "accommodating" them to new environmental conditions. Today such effects would be described as phenotypical variations or *accommodats.* Baldwin, who was thinking essentially of behavior, tried to uphold and explain the possibility of their hereditary fixation without appealing to the direct causality of the Lamarckian approach. And it was with this in mind that he developed the idea of organic selection and of what is still known today as the Baldwin effect. Clearly, Baldwin's solution, were it adequate, would be of the greatest relevance to our present purposes, for he concluded from it that "the organism itself coöperates in the formation of the adaptations which are effected,"[3] so contributing to its own selection.

Unfortunately, even though the notion of organic selection is helpful and worth retaining (provided that it is taken to embrace the selective mechanisms specific to the internal environment), Baldwin nowhere offers a convincing account of what is now described in terms of "replacement of the phenotype by a genotype," and hence in terms of "phenocopy," because the discoverer of organic selection looked upon its effects not as a replacement but rather as a gradual fixation.

2. It would perhaps be true to say that Baldwin appears to waver between these alternative interpretations, but whichever solution he favors, he leaves a number of vital questions unanswered. Here is a passage, for instance, where he indeed seems to come down on the side of fixation: Successive accommodations "permit variations orientated in the same direction to develop through subsequent generations, while variations orientated in other directions will disappear without becoming fixed. The species will thus progress in those directions first indicated and laid down by acquired modifications, and little by little traits which were originally individual acquisitions will become congenital variations. The outcome is the same as it would have been given direct heredity."[4] Yet on the very next page we read in connection with the sequence of accumulating accommodations that "during this time the species may perfect its congenital mechanism and appropriate it precisely"[5]—seemingly a clear adoption of a replacement as opposed to a fixation model.

Now, if we recall Baldwin's definition of organic selection as the survival of those individuals that accommodate themselves,[6] the first of these passages can mean only one thing—provided we exclude Lamarckian direct causality, which is Baldwin's explicit intent. What it means, to put it in modern terms, is that the individuals that accommodate themselves retain only a part of the genotype's reaction range, and that when these accommodations persist through succeeding generations, it will always be the phenotypical reactions that will be repeated. But if a phenotype thus manages to achieve stabilization as such—i.e., without becoming hereditary—the genotype will nevertheless have undergone no variations, and its reaction range, though exploited in one sector only, will preserve its other possibilities. Thus, the selection of *accommodats* in no way implies any hereditary "fixation." Indeed, this situation may obtain indefinitely, witness the nonoccurrence of genetic transmission of native languages in the human species.

However, the second passage, in which Baldwin asserts that as individual accommodations are repeated generation after generation "the species can perfect its congenital mechanism," appears to be saying something quite different and, specifically, positing a process of "replacement" rather than one of fixation. We may readily grant that phenotypical accommodations and the forms of behavior characterizing them are necessary to survival while the "congenital mechanism" is being "perfected." On the other hand, it is hard to see—short of reverting to Lamarck—why this perfecting process should be determined by the perfecting of the accommodats. In fact, aside from considerations of speed, there is no reason, according to the terms of Baldwin's account, why it should not come about quite independently of them.

The fact is, no doubt, that Baldwin failed to see that the two approaches were contradictory. He must have assumed that by selecting only a portion of the reaction norm, the accommodations became the form of behavior responsible for the "perfecting" of the "congenital mechanism." But this is not proven. Quite the reverse: experience shows that among cases of seemingly stable phenotypes, some lose their characteristics with the return to an old environment (e.g., the small phenotypical *Sedum album* living above an altitude of 2,000 meters), whereas others retain them (e.g., a few rare populations in Savoie transplanted to low altitudes). Only in the latter cases does true "replacement" by a new genotype occur. The nonuniversality of the phenocopy is thus a powerful argument against the over-simple mechanisms that Baldwin ascribed to his "organic selection." Thus, in the sphere of animal behavior, habits may recur generation after generation without heredity playing any role, especially where such habits are reinforced by mimetic or learning factors.

3. Organic selection cannot produce the results Baldwin would wish unless it is first seen as linked to the internal environment, unless we assume that the internal

environment is modified by it before proceeding to select and canalize mutations. As a matter of fact, Baldwin
was quite familiar with this process of "intraselection,"
and he allotted it a place in his general table of types of
selection,[7] referring in this connection to Roux's "strug-
gle between the parts." But he fails to perceive its necessary link with organic selection. Of course, new accommodations and forms of behavior brought about by
environmental changes will change the internal environment to a variable degree. In some cases the modification may be superficial, in which event the production of
accommodats will not necessarily be followed by genic
transformation. Elsewhere, adaptation to a new external
environment, along with new types of behavior, can give
rise to more or less profound imbalances capable of
changing the internal environment at more primitive hierarchical levels. And it is the new mutations made possible by such circumstances (whether or not they are
related to the imbalance—a question we shall discuss in
Chapter Six) which become subject to selection by the
internal environment, and hence to a sort of endo-adaptation. Now, since this environment has been transformed in conjunction with the formation of the phenotype, there is nothing surprising about the fact that the
new mutations selected by the modified internal environment "mimic" this phenotype. Under such conditions,
therefore, we have replacement not fixation—a replacement, furthermore, which is due to a process of endogenous reconstruction affected in no way by the direct action of the exogenous factors characteristic of the
external environment. Clearly, this conformity between
the new hereditary behavior and the phenotypical ac-

commodations that have preceded it and even indirectly given rise to it cannot be explained in terms of selections unless Baldwin's organic selection and what he calls intraselection are treated as an indivisible whole, with the internal environment supplying the necessary causal mediation between the two successive formative processes. The Baldwin effect is indeed interpreted today in a comparable way, but the important point is that Baldwin's organic selection does not of itself furnish an adequate explanation of the process of phenocopy.

4. Despite Baldwin's somewhat over-hasty conclusion that "we now see how individual or ontogenetic accommodations may be transformed into progress in the race,"[8] the fact remains that organic selection has a fundamental role in evolution in its own right, and quite independently of whatever part it plays in the more complex mechanisms of phenocopy. Generally speaking, and even beyond the sphere of behavior in the strict sense, a species' ability to adapt by means of simple accommodations which conform afresh to phenotypical patterns with each new generation without benefit of hereditary transmission suffices to guarantee this species a very stable survival. Thus, an Alpine plant may ensure the survival of its species in a phenotypically determined form just as effectively as if this form were hereditary. Similarly, *Limnaea ovata* inhabiting abyssal regions of Lake Léman perpetuate their race by means of accommodations so atypical that several authors including myself at first took them for a distinct species, until it was discovered that their descendants born in an aquarium com-

pletely lost the characteristics of the deep-water varieties and became quite indistinguishable from littoral specimens.

As for the specific sphere of behavior, the general tendency toward the extension of the environment mentioned above is clearly a function of organic selection because what is involved initially is an aggregation of individual initiatives. Therefore, independently of heredity, and given the fact of an equal rate of reproduction at the outset, the importance of this factor in relation to the evolutionary destiny of species is obvious. An additional striking fact is that in mastering a new environment a species will very often increase its coefficient of reproduction. This is true, for instance, of *Xerophila obvia,* already cited in Chapter One, or of the Turkish turtledove which has recently invaded Western Europe and which reproduces in the Genevan countryside at a rate far superior to that achieved by the wood pigeon. In short, the utility of the notion of organic selection lies in the fact that it brings out the organism's active collaboration in the selection process without limiting us to the idea of a sorting procedure imposed by the environment alone. Another original aspect of Baldwin's approach worth embracing is his thesis that a good proportion of the accommodations destined to initiate new genotypes are the outcome of initiatives taken during ontogenesis, and that these initiatives are not preformed but constitute genuine innovations, albeit based on congenital structures in which they precipitate variations.[9]

The sources of organic selection must thus be sought as far back as ontogenesis, especially in cases where there is a need to deal with those disturbances which serve to keep the organism in a state of vital activity and which provoke responses undetermined by pre-existing hereditary programming pending the refinement of this programming. Such pedogenesis, as it has since been called, is often evoked by more recent authors.

Notes to Chapter Two

1. James M. Baldwin, *Mental Development in the Child and the Race* (1894). Reprint of third revised edition of 1906 (New York: Augustus M. Kelly, 1968), p. 192.

2. Ibid., p. 194.

3. Baldwin, "A New Factor in Evolution," *American Naturalist* (1896), p. 553.

4. Baldwin, *Le développement mental chez l'enfant et dans la race* (1897), p. 181. [This passage and later ones are from a section that does not appear in the English-language editions of Baldwin's *Mental Development in the Child and the Race—trans.*]

5. Ibid., p. 182.

6. Baldwin, *Social and Ethical Interpretations in Mental Development* (1897).

7. Ibid.

8. Baldwin, *Développement mental*, p. 186.

9. Baldwin, "A New Factor," section 4, p. 449.

THREE

The Ethological View of Behavior's Role in Evolution

IN THE CONTEXT of his ideas on natural selection, Darwin naturally attributed a great deal of importance to behavior as a factor in survival and in the reproduction of the species; but, aside from his interest in the phylogenetic sources of emotional expression, he never really studied habits and instincts in detail. And, despite his tardy acceptance of certain Lamarckian notions, he paid scant attention to the question of the relationship between the behavior of animals and the origin of morphological variations, except for the fact that he noted behavior's tendency to transcend its own limitations.

With the turn of the century, and the beginnings of neo-Darwinism, this attitude was considerably modified by two developments. The first was the introduction and general acceptance of the notion of mutation, conceived of as a rapid, endogenous, and entirely fortuitous variation. Deemed the only possible point of origin of evolutionary transformations, the mutation was now called upon to account for the genesis of hereditary behavior as well as that of morphological changes. Thus, as Simpson writes, "In extreme form, [these] views practically eliminated behavior as an essential element in evolution"[1] because they ascribed the adaptation of even the most specialized instincts solely to an *a posteriori* selection process designed to retain those mutations most favorable to survival and reproduction.

The second important new departure was the development of ethology, which, on the contrary, has tended to point up the part played by behavior ever more clearly. To quote Simpson again, ethology "reinstates behavior not merely as something to which evolution has happened but as something that is itself one of the essential determinants of evolution."[2] But the net effect of neo-Darwinism's ever-expanding influence on the one hand and the considerable headway made by ethology on the other has been an extremely paradoxical situation, which needs to be dealt with in some detail.

1. Let us first recall the pairs of problems raised by the question of the relationship between behavior and evolution, and by explanations of the two forms of adaptation manifested by instinctive or other kinds of behavior. With regard to the first point, the relationship between behavior and evolution, the two aspects that have to be distinguished—and this even at the most elementary level—are behavior's role in selection, which has always been universally recognized (though opinions differ as to its importance), and its possible role in the actual formation of evolutionary variations. This second role, the postulation of which seemed obviously correct to Lamarck and just as obviously wrong—even absurd— to orthodox neo-Darwinists, is only now beginning to be

debated once more. As for the adaptation of behavior to the specific environment to which it corresponds, here too there are two problems to be distinguished. The first is that of global adaptation or survival (by which is meant the favorable reproduction of the species or population as much as the survival of individuals). The second is that of the differentiated adaptation which I propose to call adequation. This presupposes a detailed correspondence or morphism (in the mathematical sense) between particular organs or movements of the organism and specific aspects of the environment or of objects affected by the action in question: for example, the adequation of an insect's sting or probe to the integument of its victim or to the morphological disposition of flowers; the adequation of a triton's instinctive movements as it folds a leaf around its eggs; and so on.[3]

Now, it so happens that a good many ethologists, out of fidelity to the neo-Darwinist position, attribute an evolutionary role to behavior solely at the level of selection, and not at the level of the actual formation of hereditary variations, despite the close kinship between so many specialized organs and their behavioral functioning; the origins of both, in other words, may be accounted for entirely in terms of chance, and the teleonomic perfection we witness in the end result must thus be ascribed exclusively to selections made after the fact. As for these selections themselves, the very remarkable contributions of contemporary ethology are naturally concerned as much with adequations as with survival mechanisms, if not more so. But ethology really only deals with the *results* of these adequations, which it studies in minute detail under the rubric of "matching," and not with their formative mechanisms, since every formation and every variation, with the sole exception of "differential" reproduction (increase in the rate of proliferation), is attributed to chance. It seems, therefore, that ethology as conceived of by the majority of its present-day practitioners raises more questions than it answers. And while I have no wish to belittle ethology's achievements, there is no call, in connection with the problems that concern us here and especially in view of the criticisms of Paul A. Weiss and several others, for us to abandon a stringent examination of the ethological position in favor of a passive and over-respectful attitude toward it.

2. The posture of those ethologists who espouse orthodox neo-Darwinism is exemplified in a particularly paradoxical way in an excellent article by C. S. Pittendrigh in the collective work *Behavior and Evolution*. Pittendrigh sets out by maintaining, quite rightly, that there is no reciprocity between environment and organism within the adaptation process, in that "the essential nonrandomness of adaptation is due entirely to the organism's (not the environment's) capacity to accumulate and retain information both phylogenetic and ontogenetic."[4] He then proceeds to stress adaptation's teleonomic nature and its kinship with organization. Organization, too, he treats as fundamentally "nonrandom"; as the opposite of disorder and chance, organization represents an improbable state of affairs in a purely contingent universe, an "information content" based on negative entropy. The basic problem for Pittendrigh is thus the origin of the information that underpins and causes such organization: "How has the information content of the genotype accumulated in the face of the universal tendency to maximize entropy [i.e., disorganization]?"[5] One gets the impression from such remarks that Pittendrigh is basing his theories on notions akin to Weiss's "hierarchical system," with its two essential characteristics: the whole has greater stability than the parts; and local or partial variations are controlled by hierarchically superior agencies. Yet, after formulating the general problems with such clarity, Pittendrigh proceeds to assert that the only possible solution to these problems is the Darwinian conception of natural selection, and that the innovations which follow one another in the course of evolution are attributable solely to processes of mutation and recombination.[6] In other words, the nonrandom character of organization and of the adaptations organization brings about are to be ascribed to the genetic conservation of an "accumulation" of small variations that have been appropriately sorted out by means of selection, but every one of which owes its existence entirely to chance. The inconsistency of this account is flagrant: the organized and adaptable whole constituted by the living organism is said to be a nonrandom system that is nevertheless the outcome of a conservation mechanism affecting aggregates of selected minor traits whose genesis is purely a matter of chance. It is true, of course, that selection may have been responsible for retaining only the most desirable traits; but it has not *produced* these traits. We are asked to conceive of selection on the analogy of a consumer who not only chooses a desirable commodity among those offered, but who somehow also modifies it beforehand—and perhaps even manufactures a few himself before selecting the best of these products of his own ingenuity. In fact, one often encounters arguments seemingly based on the assumption that selection itself engenders useful properties, whereas it can really do no more than encourage the choice and preservation of such properties.[7]

Clearly, then, any discussion of the relationship between behavior and evolution in general must embrace the formation of new types of behavior as it relates to the endogenous organization and adaptation of living things. We cannot confine ourselves to the success of such types of behavior in respect to selection. In other words, we have to direct our attention to the manner in which adequations are constructed, not just to their results in "matching."

3. This is not the place for a critique of neo-Darwinism; such critiques are becoming more and more common, in any case. On the other hand, it is important to point up the particular difficulty encountered by those who wish to explain the emergence of new forms of behavior in terms of the production of chance mutations. Their task is hard for two reasons. In the first place, in any piece of behavior the whole body acts upon external objects in the environment, and such actions involve movements extending beyond the somatic realm. In the second place, however, the genome contains only forms, and it could not prefigure such movements from the outset, except in terms of teleonomic programming, without the occurrence of more or less indirect interactions between the organism's epigenetic activities and the formation of mutations or their selection by the internal environment.

31

The problem arises initially over the question of temporal succession: behavioral modifications generally constitute the source of changes of ecological niches (a fact stressed notably by Mayr, also in *Behavior and Evolution*), and only subsequently does adaptation to the new environment entail structural transformations. It may even happen that without any change of environment specific movements will appear phylogenetically in advance of the morphological structures destined to invest them with meaning. Thus, Konrad Lorenz has shown that many birds raise the feathers of the head or back of the neck and incline this part of their bodies toward females or rivals. Now, some species—but some only— have developed long crests which accentuate such movements and seem to have resulted from them. In other cases, by contrast, it is the structural change which appears to have come about first. In his article on the genetic basis of behavior, in the same collective work, Caspari maintains that in insects a gene may be selected because of its "pleiotropic effect" on behavior, although its principal action is upon morphological characteristics.

These facts raise two questions of fundamental importance in connection with behavior's role in evolution. Should the genesis of behavior turn out to precede morphological change, the preliminary question which we shall of course have to ask is whether behavior is the result from the outset of a mutation (and thus hereditary from the start, though having a chance-governed origin), or whether it has been preceded by phenotypical accommodations (either in adulthood or during epigenesis) and has subsequently given rise to a phenocopy which has become hereditary, though only after a process of genetic reconstruction. Now, despite all the emphasis that has been laid on the rigidity of instinctive movements in insects, we know for instance that the wasp *Ammophile urnaris* displays great variation in the way in which individuals build their nests and bring caterpillars to them on which to lay their eggs. Such plasticity is obviously a propitious seeding-ground for the establishment of the phenotypes of many behavioral forms. Admittedly, all phenotypes remain under genetic control within the limits of what is called a reaction norm, but it is important to draw a careful distinction when dealing with such norms between what is truly "determined" by the genome and variations due to superior subsystems, interacting with the surroundings, which are consistent with the norm merely because of their "compatibility" with specific traits of the genome and not because they are determined by it.[8]

The second major problem raised by the various possible relationships between behavioral changes and structural or morphological variations has to do with the nature of coadaptation between genes, given that several genes may be involved in the formation of a single trait ("polygeny"), while one gene may affect several traits at once ("pleiotropism"). Even more urgently than isolated variations, coordination of this kind in genic action raises the crucial question of the respective roles of chance on the one hand and possible organizational or regulatory factors on the other. For, difficult as it is to be satisfied with an explanation of adaptive modifications in behavior couched in terms of an *a posteriori* selection of random mutations in isolatable genes, when it comes to the reorganization of the combined effects of several genes acting in concert, this type of approach is even more untenable, and the need to think in terms of a combination of factors becomes overwhelming. As Weiss asks, how can "discrete units" such as genes achieve organization (and this at all levels) unless they are "enmeshed in, and in interplay with, an organized reference system of unified dynamics of the collective of which they are the members."[9] This second problem has thus led us back to the first, for the postulation of an overall dynamic of this kind implies that at the source of all coordination between structures and forms of behavior a part must be played by hierarchically superior systems whose activity sooner or later affects the genome. But how does this happen? I will try to answer this question in Chapter Six and Chapter Seven.

4. The two problems we have just discussed have to be formulated rather differently according to the type of variation under consideration, however, so let us now review the different kinds of variations in the context of the formation of behavior. A first distinction is that between quantitative and qualitative variations. Quantitative variations consist simply in the strengthening or weakening of a given trait. We find great differences, for instance, in the rate of learning for rats of different breeds (cf., the work of Bovet and others), or in degrees of aggression, or affectivity, or motor activity, and so on. Such modifications, sometimes the outcome of spontaneous mutations in known loci, are naturally the easiest to explain in terms of chance and of selection after the fact. But the problem becomes markedly more complex

as soon as we turn our attention to such qualitative variations as the very different courting motions of birds of
closely related species. For instance, the posture
adopted by young birds of the family *Nesomimus* when
soliciting food varies from one island to the next in the
Galapagos. The role of selection in this situation is hard
to see; for, since the environments are clearly separated
from one another, competition can play no part. On the
contrary, one gets the impression that a kind of combinatory system[10] operates here, tending to exhaust all the
variations possible on the basis of the same initial pattern.

In addition, three types of cases are to be distinguished among qualitative variations. The first type corresponds to what were classically known as orthogeneses
—i.e., successive variations tending in the same direction. Neo-Darwinians no longer believe in orthogenesis
except where cumulative selective actions occur. In the
famous case of Neumayr's *Vivipara,* however, we have an
incontestable instance of orthogenesis where it is impossible to discern the slightest trace of a selective factor.
What are involved here are simply slight changes of form
in the shells which, rounded to begin with, become more
and more markedly spiraled. A fact which makes this
phenomenon even more remarkable, first observed in
Slavonian beds of paludal mollusks, is that it recurred in
paleontological findings from the island of Kos in the
Dodecanese.[11] The second type of qualitative variation
is characterized by the apparent operation of a combinatory system of the kind just discussed, where different
possible variations occur in closely related species. In the
third type, the most interesting, different simultaneous

variations are linked by a sort of affinity of meaning, which might almost be described as an internal logic. Thus, Hinde and Tinbergen[12] describe the complex behavior peculiar to the kittiwake *(Rissa tridactyla)*, the only gull to build its nest on steep cliffs, as follows. The adult birds are less fearful, or tamer, than others. They do not attack predators, and they defecate around the nest despite the white and clearly apparent ring which this habit produces. Indeed they make no attempt to camouflage either their eggs or their young. The young themselves do not run at their parents' alarm calls, so avoiding falls. For the same reason, they do not fight among themselves over food but discourage competitors in this domain by means of characteristic neck motions revealing a black band whose significance is immediately recognized. We thus have a coherent system of a quasi-"implicative" kind, whose establishment would be highly improbable without the intervention of initial learning and phenocopy mechanisms.

5. The constant attempts to refine the explanation by Darwinian selection have nevertheless produced a useful distinction, much stressed by Mayr, between the selection of optimal behavior, a factor of uniformity, and a selection that fosters variability, a factor of plasticity. But, aside from the dubious merit of the tautologous equation "selection = survival = reproductive capacity," the value of this distinction lies, above all, not in its evocation of a sorting process imposed by the external environment but rather in that of formative mechanisms depending, on the one hand, on relations between the variations observed and the processes of ontogenetic development and, on the other hand, on selective action effected by the internal environment, which undergoes more or less profound changes during the post-embryonic phase of ontogenesis. Although Sperry tells us (in his article on ontogenesis in the same work) that most mutations responsible for new types of behavior affect the course of development, the question still open is to what extent does development itself exert an influence in the opposite direction.

This brings us back to the central problem of the origin of new kinds of behavior. Mayr should be given credit for stating this problem in the clearest possible terms. According to him, there are only two possibilities. The first is that the new behavior has a genetic basis from the start, since any factor which modifies the hereditary traits of the species can also affect behavior—in fact, behavior may even be an accidental subproduct of genes selected on the basis of quite other properties. The second possibility is that the new behavior results from a nongenetic modification of already existing behavior (through learning, conditioning, etc.) and is then "replaced (by an unknown process) by genetically controlled behavior" (*Biology and Evolution,* p. 354). Let us now look a little more closely at these two hypotheses. The question of the nature of the phenocopy here referred to as an "unknown process" and as "genetically obscure" (pp. 354–55) I shall return to in Chapter Six.

According to the first hypothesis, then, the new behavior is the outcome of mutations, these either being viable from the start or else proving viable after selection. The new behavior's origin is thus random by definition, and its insertion into an ecological niche which is suited to it and which offers it a sufficient possibility of survival is also more or less fortuitous. Two chance occurrences, quite independent of one another, are therefore postulated at the outset. A structural modification (of an organ) may occur too, stemming in its turn from random mutations and selective adjustments also involving chance. But even granted these two additional fortuitous events, a measure of correlation still has to be established between the behavioral transformation and the adaptation of the morphological structure. Now, while already accommodated behavior must obviously make an important contribution to the selection process which eventually stabilizes or even canalizes such structural mutations, the fact remains that the problem is very different depending on whether it is a matter simply of coordinating the two selections or adaptations of the "survival" type which ensure the success of the two (behavioral and structural) modifications and of their coexistence; or whether an account has to be given also of their adaptation according to the adequation type (see #1 above), which would imply a much tighter link— indeed a necessary one—between the behavior in question and its structural organ. And since we are indeed confronted with the task of identifying and explaining this adequation of the morphological structure and of behavior to a specific milieu, along with that of this structure to the behavior that corresponds to it, the unlikelihood of this twofold adequation occurring in this way is immediately obvious, because of the great number of factors both random and unconnected which would all have to come into play: multiplicative probability decreases with increase in the number of variables. As for the suggestion that behavioral and structural variations are linked from the outset owing to coadaptation of the genes responsible, this thesis undoubtedly leads us out of the realm of chance and even tends to imply a regulation of combinations of mutations—a position that has been defended by various authors but cannot be described as an orthodox neo-Darwinian one.

Coming now to the second hypothesis, let us suppose that the new behavior, constituted at the beginning of the sequence "behavior → choice of niche → structural modification," takes in the first instance—and notably during epigenesis—phenotypical form only. This account evokes a very different situation from the earlier hypothesis and poses problems no less complex. But at least it does not make chance solely responsible for producing more and more subtle, quasi-"intelligent"—and thus less and less probable—solutions, leaving selection as the mere arbiter of the success or failure of these at a later time. The three great advantages of treating behavior as generated phenotypically are the following: (a) Accommodation to the new environment "chosen" by the organism and the modification of behavior designed to facilitate this accommodation become contemporaneous and conjoined processes. (b) This adaptation comes to be seen as a form of adequation which naturally fosters survival but which also effects more or less complex correspondences between the new behavior and specific aspects of the environment, thus making the accommodation process more differentiated and more efficient. (c) A direct link is established between the new behavior and at least the beginnings of structural change. Such change at this stage is also purely phenotypical, of

39

course, but this view reduces the role of chance to a minimum. Needless to say, such phenotypical adaptations may remain at this stage from generation to generation without giving way to genotypes, so that no evolutionary progress occurs in the sense of modification of the genome. It is also possible, on the other hand, that the phenotype will sooner or later be "replaced" by genotypes which imitate it (phenocopy), or which even go beyond it to a greater or lesser extent by virtue of new combinations among adapted genes. These are the processes which Baldwin sought to explain with his organic selection, which Waddington attributes to "genetic assimilation," and which we shall be looking at more closely below.

Although this approach implies a new emphasis on the effects—or at any rate the indirect effects—of the environment, it is very important to note (and we shall be returning to this point again and again) that it is the consideration of the internal environment and of changes which may occur therein under the influence of new phenotypes which makes it possible for us to envisage a simultaneous transcendence of Lamarckianism and neo-Darwinism. For the internal environment clearly also plays a part in selection: changes in it are on this reading at once more or less direct *effects* of the external world, brought about through the mediation of the phenotype (the Lamarckian factor), and *causes* of the selection of mutations occurring at the same time more or less randomly (the Darwinian factor). There is one great difference, however, between intraselection applied to mutations by the internal environment and the selective capacity to which external conditions are of necessity limited; this latter capacity applies only to survival and to the differential rate of reproduction of the species (along, of course, with any resulting recombinations), whereas intraselection has the possibility of becoming a factor in adequation. Indeed, this type of selection occurs at every level of epigenetic synthesis, starting with the primitive interactions of germinative cells with plasma. Consequently, to the extent that new phenotypes have modified the internal environment, they give rise to a sort of selective framework whose action is already morphogenetic in character in that it is informed by the way in which these phenotypes have been constituted through epigenetic changes. The phenotypes are accommodated to the external surroundings thanks to a direct activity on the part of the organism, an activity which aims at adequation since it consists of orientated behavior and not random variations. Even where the mutations that emerge in this context are themselves the product of chance factors alone, the process of intraselection is governed by an adaptive mechanism much more accurate than selection attributable solely to the external world, because it embodies constant adjustments carried out by means of epigenetic regulation.

The operation of such a mechanism depends, of course, upon the extent of the changes wrought by the phenotype on the internal environment, which is why most phenotypes never give way to analogous genotypes. On the other hand, where extensive change or disturbance does occur, the question of the degree of chance involved arises (and we shall discuss it later), and of the possibility of a "regulation of mutations" as envisaged by both L. L. Whyte and Britten and Davidson. Most importantly, the question of the unknown "processes" evoked by Mayr in connection with phenocopy will arise, processes which are even more obscure when it comes to the formation of differentiated instincts.

Notes to Chapter Three

1. A. Rowe and G. G. Simpson, eds., *Behavior and Evolution* (New Haven: Yale University Press, 1958), p. 8.

2. Ibid., p. 9.

3. This distinction between overall adaptations gauged solely by the yardstick of survival and "adequations" of detail between a given form of behavior and some specific aspect of the environment can only be meaningful in the context of exchange between organism and environment. For, clearly, the internal processes of the organism—from the coadaptation of the genes, or the synthesis of proteins with their stereospecific links, to the tracks of hormones making their way to their target organs—all manifest a multiplicity of ultraprecise adequations. So true is this, indeed, that in some cases—in the case of hormonal tracks or in that of the functioning of "amoebocytes" in *Spongiae*—one is almost tempted to speak in terms of the organism's "internal behavior."

4. Ibid., p. 391.

5. Ibid., pp. 396–97.

6. Recombination is the product of the genes of the two parents in sexual reproduction.

7. Thus Pittendrigh writes in *Behavior and Evolution* that "A given problem—a given pattern of selection—is met by a multiplicity of different solutions in different (and even in the same) organism" (p. 400)—as though these solutions were somehow devised by selection itself.

8. Cf., Weiss's distinction between those characteristics which are "gene-determined" and those which are merely "gene-related." See Paul A. Weiss, "The Basic Concept of

Hierarchic Systems," in Weiss *et al.*, *Hierarchically Organized Systems in Theory and Practice* (New York: Hafner, 1971), p. 34.

9. Ibid., p. 38.

10. As distinct from "recombinations" associated with sexual reproduction. I shall return to this question in Chapter Seven.

11. See *Denkschr. Akad.-Wissensch.* (Vienna, 1880), vol. 40, pp. 213–314.

12. In *Behavior and Evolution.*

———⚬⚭⚬———

FOUR

Cybernetic Interaction, "Genetic Assimilation," and Behavior

BEHAVIOR'S ROLE in the formative mechanisms of evolution was naturally reinterpreted in a more comprehensive fashion once it was realized that biological causality is never linear or atomistic in form, but always implies the operation of feedback systems as defined by the cyberneticians. The postulation of this mode of operation not only conferred a causal or mechanical character on teleonomy—it also meant that interactions had to be taken into consideration everywhere one-way causality had formerly been deemed an adequate explanatory model. But for a long time there was one case to which this general rethinking was not applied—namely, the process whereby DNA becomes RNA. For some reason, nobody questioned the idea that this process was unidirectional and irreversible. We know enough now, however, thanks to the work of Temin and others, to say that it may be reversed on occasion.

1. In this context it was natural enough that as early as 1960 Schmalhausen should have sought to uncover

the cybernetic underpinnings of evolutionary mechanisms, but also that he should take care to show the
customary respect for the doctrine of the purely endogenous and chance-governed origin of each new hereditary
variation. It took an author like Waddington, trained in
both embryology and genetics, to take the leap of distin-
guishing two great subsystems, genetic and "epigenetic," the first linked to the second by regulatory circuits. Waddington further ascribed the same circular
causality to the relationship between epigenesis and a
third subsystem, the "exploitation of the environment,"
as well as to that between this last and a fourth, constituted by the entirety of the operations of natural selection.

To begin with the relationships between the behavior
of the phenotype (produced epigenetically), the exploitation of the environment, and natural selection, two
major theses of Waddington's are relevant to our present concerns. The first asserts that organisms "choose"
their environment and that the selection process thus
embodies a certain reciprocity. On the one hand, the
living organism's activity is directed toward the retention
of particular external conditions which suit it for reasons
having to do with the fueling of its patterns of action
(initially nutrition in the physiological sense; subsequently a variety of purposes). Similarly, the organism
abandons or rejects unsuitable environmental conditions. On the other hand, the environment exerts an
action fostering changes in the organism which tally with
the conditions chosen and discouraging variations unable to accommodate to these conditions. In short, the
exploitation of the environment is indeed a circular proc-

ess involving reciprocal transformations, in that organisms modify their environment (from the lowest form of plant life up through nest-building, etc.), while the environment, in turn, induces variations in organisms. The specificity of this interaction, however, lies in the fact that the organism takes advantage of the environment, whereas the environment confines itself, as it were, to placing conditions upon the organism; the whole process is nevertheless one of gradual mutual adjustment. Thus, Waddington stresses the importance of behavior by describing it as "one of the factors which determines the magnitude and type of evolutionary pressure to which the animal will be subjected. It is at the same time a producer of evolutionary change as well as a resultant of it, since it is the animal's behavior which to a considerable extent determines the nature of the environment to which it will submit itself and the character of the selective forces with which it will consent to wrestle."[1]

Waddington's second important thesis regarding selection is that it does not apply to the genes directly. It operates instead at the level of phenotypical traits, with the rider that these are nevertheless subject to "genetic control"; it is no longer a matter, as it was for Baldwin, of the simple retention of successful accommodations and the rejection of the others. For Waddington as for Dobzhansky, in fact, the phenotype is a response of the genome to the solicitations of the environment, and each of its traits remains subordinate to genotypical directives, so that the selection process, though it applies only to phenotypes, is nevertheless "taken over by the genotype."[2]

As for the nature of this control, so essential to the

mechanism of "genetic assimilation," it, too, depends on a causality of the feedback type, operating between the epigenetic system and the genome itself. And here the geneticist in Waddington takes lessons from the embryologist. According to the model of successive epigenetic syntheses which Waddington proposes,[3] the genome's polygenic and pleiotropic action is not to be envisaged in terms of simple ascent; for at each level, hitherto inactive genes (which have of course been *present* from the outset) are brought into play as the result of actions already performed by other genes. For example, the result X, produced by genes a, c, and e, activates gene b, which then works synergistically with a and d to produce the result Y, which will in turn activate other genes, and so on. What we have, then, is a feedback system that is indeed modified, at the higher levels, by the environment, because what is changed is the phenotype. But at the same time, this modification is the outcome of a selective process which is "under genic control" in that it depends on the successive syntheses for which the genome is responsible.

We are now in a position to define the central mechanism, genetic assimilation, which affects behavior as well as morphological variations, as follows. It is that process whereby a phenotypical trait, generated to begin with in response to a given environmental influence, is preserved by virtue of a selection taken over by the genotype, even in the absence of those external conditions prerequisite to its formation. This view of matters is akin to the Baldwin effect thesis—or at least to modern accounts of it—except for the essential refinement of placing selection "under genic control."

2. This approach is an attractive one—and, as a matter of fact, I adopted it myself for a time—but there is a problem with it which we have already mentioned above in other connections. This has to do with the ambiguity of the notion of genetic control and with the obscurity of the supposed transition, in each specific case, from this control to what Waddington calls the canalization of variations and of new development.

The fact is that genetic control, just as much as the eventual selection, is limited by a "reaction norm"; both result in the retention of some of the possibilities compatible with this range and the exclusion of the rest. Let us try to clarify this idea of a reaction norm. The range expresses the possible phenotypical variations acceptable to a given genotype. Suppose it comprises the traits A, B, C, etc., each of which has two aspects: the first aspect (a for A, b for B, etc.) is always present and is determined by the genes upon which it depends; the second aspect (a' for A, b' for B, etc.) is the result of environmental factors, and thus may or may not emerge depending on the surroundings, but it is invariably associated with the first, conditioning, aspect (a for a', b for b', etc.). When a given environment precipitates a variation, this must be due to the fact that particular traits are manifested or produced (e.g., A, B, and C, but not D, E, etc.). In this event, A, B, and C will each present two components *(aa', bb', cc')*. D and E, having no role, will be restricted to their genic component *(d* and *e)*, but they will remain within the genome and will not become manifest in the phenotype corresponding to the environment in question. In fact, if D, E, etc., were to emerge in this environment, the individuals presenting such traits would be eliminated and selection would retain only the bearers of A, B, and C. Up to this point, then, we follow Waddington. But two problems inevitably arise when we postulate a change of environment for the phenotypes that have been selected in this way. First, will the preserved traits A, B, and C now appear under their dual aspect $(aa', bb',$ and $cc')$ or merely under the aspect a, b, and c, though accompanied now by a new variation (a'', b'', c'') due to the new environment? Second, are the traits D and E, which had been eliminated in the earlier environment, now destined to disappear from the genome itself? Or will they remain present, and capable of manifesting themselves in the new environment in the forms dd'' and ee'', inasmuch as it is only the forms dd' and ee' which are not viable (up to now, at any rate)?

The import of these questions is obvious. They stem, once again, from the fact that the notion of genetic control remains ambiguous as long as no clear distinction is drawn between traits "determined by the genome" (i.e., a, b, c, etc.) and traits merely "compatible with the action of the genes," but influenced by the environment (i.e., a', b', c', etc.). Now, it seems to me that Waddington argues as though, when genetic selection retains the traits A, B, and C, it conserves not only their genetic aspect, a, b, and c, but also their phenotypical aspect, a', b', and c', despite the fact that this aspect is only "compatible" with the genetic component and in no sense "determined" by it. It is very hard, admittedly, to find the line of demarcation between the genic aspects *(a, b, c,* etc.) and the exogenic aspects *(a', b', c',* etc.) of a variation or phenotypical trait. But this distinction is nonetheless a logical necessity. (Weiss characterizes it by opposing "determined by the genes" to "linked to the genes.") And the best empirical proof of its validity lies in the fact that many phenotypes clearly selected as such give rise to no genotypical fixation (e.g., certain high-altitude plant and animal varieties; the abyssal *Limnaea ovata,* referred to as *profunda,* of Lake Léman; and so on). The limits to such replacements are thus legion, and the negative cases have to be accounted for as much as the apparently positive instances.

As for the second problem, that posed by the traits *D, E,* etc., which appear to be eliminated as a result of the selection of phenotypes (so that only *A, B,* and *C* are retained), there are two possible solutions here. One possibility is that their genic components *(d* and *e)* are indeed suppressed within the genome by such a selection process. The other possibility, which is in fact just as probable, is that components *d* and *e* have simply not found viable phenotypical manifestations *(d'* and *e').* This would mean that only the combinations *dd'* and *ee'* are eliminated. The selection does not eliminate the components *d* and *e* themselves, and these may still give rise, given a new environment, to viable combinations *(dd", ee").*

In short—and assuming that I have understood Waddington correctly—the notion of a selection of phenotypes "taken over by the genome" means first and foremost that only a section of the genome's "reaction norm" is retained, though at the same time nothing guarantees the elimination of the other sections, which may persist *in potentia*, ready to emerge given a change in environment, witness the innumerable cases where the phenotype fails to initiate a new genotype.

3. But Waddington's cybernetic approach is so fruitful that the circuits he posits, notably his picture of the links between the epigenetic system and the genome itself, supply us with a host of refinements which we must now examine in order to see whether they can resolve the difficulties we have just outlined. The first of these refinements is Waddington's most helpful account of the "multidimensional" nature of the environment or environments which exert an influence during the selection processes: the external and internal environments; the epigenetic environment; and so on. In addition to these spatial dimensions, Waddington also postulates the existence of a temporal one. Secondly, he rightly stresses the fact that selection does not only affect static characteristics, but also the genome's degree of "sensitivity" to exogenic disturbing factors. These considerations give us the wherewithal to explain the formation of new genotypes mimicking phenotypes influenced by the external environment, provided always (see Chapter Six) that selection is seen as governed by an internal environment modified by the phenotypes themselves and not simply subordinated to genetic control.

A third point of Waddington's, by contrast, is something of an oversimplification. As early as 1942 he was suggesting that thanks to "natural selection" alone all the necessary genetic "machinery" existed to "reproduce any given environmental effect which was of value to the animal concerned."[4] But, in fact, a choice has to be made. Either selection (in the usual sense) is simply a procedure for making choices and not an organizing force, in which case the new genotype is the outcome solely of a predictable combination of pre-existing elements; or else new genetic combinations are formed, but if so they have to be accounted for, and it has to be decided whether selection can adequately explain such a development.

Now, the first alternative fails completely to account for the creative aspect of evolution, and most notably for the constitution of new forms of behavior capable of generating new organs, as in the case of the emergence of legs, wings, etc. Indeed, the two pitfalls to be avoided in approaching these problems are the postulation of an unmediated environmental determinism, after the fashion of Lamarck, and the overly simple hypothesis of preformation, which Waddington appears to be espousing with his all-powerful genome. But he likewise only partially resists the attraction of the verbal solution which invokes pure chance followed by sorting procedures after the fact.

So it is really to the second alternative that Waddington inclines. He believes that new genetic combinations are formed, though he holds that the ground is laid by potentialities in the genome. But the surprising thing is that at this point in his account, having accepted that such new formations occur, Waddington evokes that same "selection under genic control," whose many ambiguities we have just reviewed, and endows it with an *organizing* capacity rather than a merely *selective* one in the sense of an ability to stabilize or even canalize. More precisely, Waddington equates canalization with "combination"[5]—which is, after all, something very different.

Thus, in discussing the contraction of *Limnaea stagnalis* in the hereditary variety *lacustris,* a phenomenon so closely bound up with the animal's motor behavior, Waddington charges that I underestimate the role of selection. To back up this charge, however, he adduces two arguments which are equally instructive in connection with the reservations I have just expressed. The first appeals to a measure of predetermination. Even before selection, according to Waddington, *stagnalis* genomes already contain "many genes tending to produce the modified phenotype under the influence of the suitable environmental stress." A possibility, certainly—but unproven. The second hypothesis is that the "selection gradually brings together many different genes tending in this direction, and the combination of these genes suffices to produce" the variety *lacustris.* Thus, selection becomes the origin of unifications and combinations. Even more surprisingly, in the case of the *bodamica* varieties (maximal contraction), "selection has done more than it need[s] to, but this 'making doubly sure' is characteristic of the process of genetic assimilation."

As a matter of fact, I have no wish to deny the role of selection in such cases; I would merely insist that it be attributed to an internal environment *modified by the phenotype,* and that its operation go no further than the canalization of the genic reorganizations which result from the fact that normal hereditary programming is countered by these modifications. My term "progressive reorganization" may seem very vague to Waddington,[6] but I feel that his notion of selection as an organizing process has much more serious drawbacks. When he writes that selection "has done more than it needs to" (and it should be recalled that the nonhereditary phenotypes of the *lacustris* kind are already capable of survival), surely this is to be explained by the intervention within Waddington's "selection under genic control" of a nexus of self-regulations which extend well beyond the bounds of what is ordinarily called selection, and which tend in the direction of those combinatory systems and complementary reinforcements whose existence I have assumed in connection with the genesis of complex instincts (see Chapter Seven).

4. In sum, I naturally concur with Waddington's notion of new genic combinations (embodying the possibilities of new mutations) resulting from the unbalancing effects of a change of environment. I also concur with the ascription of selection to the internal environment as modified by a phenotypical variation, which has for its part been imposed by the external environment—in other words, selection as the result of the formation of a new "epigenetic landscape." On the other hand, I do not consider that selection is a force for "unification"; if a selection process eliminates five possibilities from a total of fifteen, it does not follow that it "gathers together" the ten others, but merely that it has "retained" them, which is not the same thing. Similarly, a change in epigenetic landscape is not due to selection as such, but rather to the action of the external environment inasmuch as this action is "compatible" with the nature of the genes (which does not imply any purely endogenous determination by these genes).

It still remains to account for the formation of new genotypes. And to speak here of the "bringing together" or "combination" of genes which already "tend" in the appropriate direction is quite inaccurate. For the central factor is not a convergence of this kind but rather a conflict or imbalance between epigenesis as modified by the external environment and the previous genic programming, between a new setting and variations which have already been produced but which no longer suffice to ensure adjustment to the surroundings. Thus, there is no alternative to assigning some role to variations that do not pre-exist. This implies no necessity to invoke a positive or coded message informing the genome of what is occurring on the level of the higher epigenetic syntheses, which would be a regression to Lamarckianism. We need merely take it that the effects of the disequilibrium running counter to the normal unfolding of the regulatory genes gradually spread, until these genes become sensitized to them.[7] (Waddington himself draws attention to the variable "sensitivity" of the genome.) Variations of many different orientations will be produced, and it is then that a selection process attributable to the "epigenetic environment" will canalize these variations until the conflict has been resolved. But it is important to remember that selection can do no more than choose and channel, that it cannot produce anything itself. The true cause of successful innovations is the genome's union with the regulatory systems of epigenesis, systems which are at the same time sources of internal selections. Thus, although in a downward or retroactive direction these systems' feedbacks can only signal failures, in an upward or proactive one they engender a series of trial forms among which only those that successfully counter the initial disequilibrium, the starting point of this whole regulatory process, will be retained. The reason for this is that while the genome produces inheritable variations when a disturbance originating at any given level of the epigenetic system is transmitted to it, these responses are gradually adjusted by means of "trials" which give more or less favorable results. And of these trials, only those whose acceptance is guaranteed by the regulations specific to earlier stages will become fixed in heredity. In short, between ungoverned (or insufficiently governed) genic variations and a selection which chooses the best of them, we have to interpolate the processes of compensatory adjustment which transform these variations into trial forms. Now, since an analogous process is to be found at each level (and since its functional equivalent even constitutes the basic principle of the equilibration of behaviors), it is not surprising that the new genotype arising from an internal disequilibrium takes on the same form as the initial phenotype, for a convergence comes about between the adjustments which have accommodated this phenotype to the external environment and those which adapt genic variations to the epigenetic environment. This convergence results from the fact that it is indeed the phenotype itself and its external determinants (environment) which have modified the epigenetic environment and triggered the formative disequilibrium. In order to support these theses, however, we shall do well to base our discussion from the outset on those notions, more thoroughly emancipated from neo-Darwinism, which Weiss has developed out of the idea of *system.*

Notes to Chapter Four

1. C. H. Waddington, *The Evolution of an Evolutionist* (Ithaca, New York: Cornell University Press, 1975), p. 170.
2. Ibid., p. 91.
3. Waddington, *The Strategy of the Genes* (London: Allen and Unwin, 1957), Fig. 6.
4. Waddington, *Evolution of an Evolutionist*, p. 23.
5. Ibid., p. 95.
6. Ibid.
7. This would apply either to specific genes or to the genome as a whole viewed from the point of view of its global regulatory functions.

FIVE

Behavior and Weiss's Hierarchy of Systems

1. It is often forgotten that Paul A. Weiss's well-known ideas on the hierarchy of systems originate from a thesis he presented on the behavior of the vanessas in 1922,[1] at a time when the study of animal behavior was dominated by Loeb's atomistic mechanism. It was Loeb's view that any piece of simple behavior could be reduced to a tropism, and all complex forms to a mere combination of such links, the tropism itself being characterized simply as the direct effect of an external factor (e.g., light) upon the animal's movements. Weiss, while acknowledging the possibility in some cases of linear chains of movements coordinated according to a necessary sequence, contested the generality of this pattern. After close study of the behavior of the *Vanessae,* a genus of butterflies, and especially of the factors involved in these butterflies' choice of conditions for resting, Weiss concluded that all behavior was subordinate to the structure of "systems." A system in Weiss's sense is defined primarily by the existence of a "unitary totality," and it is

59

the system's overall dynamic which determines reactions, even in the case of linear chains. It is further characteristic of a system that it has the capacity to respond to an exogenous change in a state of equilibrium by an endogenous reaction tending to produce a fresh equilibrium.

In this connection it is worth citing a few of Weiss's observations on the choice of a suitable resting situation among vanessas. First of all, the butterfly moves toward the top of a wall, climbing if the surface is rough, flying if it is smooth. Next, it turns around so that its head is pointed downward. Last comes the animal's adjustment of its position in function of light sources. Where there is only one such source, the body is oriented toward the light and the head turned away; if there are two or more sources, an intermediate position is taken up, the aim being in all cases that the two eyes be exposed to an equal—but minimal—amount of light. These reactions are not manifested right after emergence from the chrysalis but arise gradually as a function of mnemic consolidation. Where light and gravity are at odds, the butterfly's position will be diagonal to the parallelogram of these two vectors. Weiss describes the animal's final posture as consistent with the minimization of energy discharged, although the preparatory activity is clearly quite costly in this regard. Thus, Weiss was able to show, not only in respect of this whole procedure, but also in respect of the butterfly's reactions to disturbances (slight movements of the wings and head, and so on), that much more is involved here than a mere submission to mechanical conditions. As early as 1922, then, his account foreshadowed the ethological studies of complex systems which are so numerous today.

Hence, there is no need to stress the way in which Weiss justifies his notion of behavior as "system reactions," so long as his observations are placed in the context of the overall behavior of animals. What is of interest for our purposes, by contrast, is, first, the generalization of his thesis to higher or truly cognitive activity, and, secondly, the transposition of these specific systems, constituted by all kinds of behavior, to the whole set of hierarchical systems and subsystems which characterize the organism.

2. With regard to the higher forms of behavior, Weiss published an interesting article in 1960 on the "biological" aspects of scientific knowledge when compared with a growth process.[2] Weiss's central notion here is that rational understanding is not the result of an accumulation of facts; facts only constitute "nutrients" which have to be "assimilated" before a coherent "system" can arise. Weiss gives a table representing the isomorphism between organic growth founded on nutrition and the development of experimental knowledge viewed as the conceptual assimilation of exogenous data. This parallel is so close to what I have always argued apropos of cognitive assimilation that there is no need for me to press the point here. It is true, of course, that in the light of the epistemic results of these general processes of integration—an integration as much organic as mental—the notions of system and of equilibration are clearly inescapable, but the interesting point for us is to see what sort of a neurological underpinning Weiss provides for such notions.

Weiss evokes three basic facts in this connection. First, such a multiplicity of elements that a structure of an atomistic kind based on simple inter-unit relationships would result in chaos; in other words, an overall dynamic is required. Second, a perpetual flux at all levels excluding models of static storage (engrams, etc.) but imposing the overriding necessity for constant reconstructions or, in other words, for reversible restructuring processes capable of ordering this $\pi\nu\tau\alpha$ $\rho\tilde{\epsilon}\iota$. And third, the loss of unreplaced components (cells and interconnections) with no apparent ill effects, which implies the existence of a set of dynamic compensations.

Apropos of the first two of these points, Weiss showed in 1969[3] that, although the human brain contains about 10^{10} cells—or 10^{15} macromolecules—and although each of these cells has an average of 10^4 connections with other brain cells, it is nevertheless a fact that, despite each cell's conservation of its individuality, its macromolecules are replaced 10^4 times in the course of life. Even at the level of the cell, therefore, we are already confronted by "systems." For each cell—to use the definition of these "totalities" formulated by Weiss on the basis of his first researches—

$$Vs \ll \Sigma \ (va + vb + vc + \ldots + vn)$$

What this means is that the number of variations of the system as a unified whole (i.e. Vs) is much less than the sum of partial variations within this whole ($va \ldots vn$). That every cell conserves its properties despite the continuous process of metabolic change which is constantly renewing its macromolecular substance constitutes a first remarkable datum. A second one is that a highly magnified film of the content of nerve cells and of their connections reveals the quite unexpected sight of perpetual, more or less periodic, peristaltic movements of forms, movements within which it seems impossible to identify fixed points that could constitute those mnemic "traces" normally deemed a necessary precondition of the conservation needed by thought processes. Since intercellular connections number about 10^4, it is obvious that the coherence and stability of the brain's cognitive activity (from primitive mnemic mechanisms to the most systematic deductive inferences) are the result not of static conservations but of constant dynamic reconstructions.

Here the second characteristic of the structure of systems becomes evident. If the whole varies less than the parts, which are in constant flux, it follows that this whole must embody an "overall dynamic" with the power to integrate and orient. It is to this dynamic that we must refer, and not to an exclusively molecular and intermolecular model, if we wish to account for what happens, first within the cell, but also and more importantly within the well-nigh inextricable tangle of the 10^4 intercellular connections. Weiss, of course, does not question the usefulness of studying the molecular level, but he expresses this essential reservation: ". . . there is no phenomenon in a living system that is *not* molecular, but there is none that is *only* molecular."[4] Hence, the necessity, constantly underlined by Weiss, for two complementary perspectives, or, more exactly, for "a dualistic concept according to which discrete units (molecules, macromolecular complexes . . .) are enmeshed in . . . an organized reference system of unified dynamics of the collective of which they are the members."[5]

But what are units for Weiss? He distinguishes three kinds: those which show constant regularities, as in a crystal; those which combine according to different sequences, like the letters in a word; and those which correspond to "a standard pattern of behavior of the component that yields recurrently the same unitary result even though there is no geometric similitude among the constellations of the components from moment to moment."[6] It is these units of the third type (which cannot be reduced to either of the first two, though many authors have sought to do precisely this) that for Weiss constitute systems.

This clarifies the third basic fact emphasized by Weiss in connection with cerebral processes. Although the brain loses an average of about 10^7 cells in a lifetime, along with about 10^{11} interconnections, its behavior suffers not at all, except in the event of senile deterioration. Whence the third major characteristic of systems, the first being the relative conservation of the whole (i.e., the relative weakness of Vs in the equation given above), and the second being the resulting unified dynamics: "A system could . . . be defined as a complex unit in space and time so constituted that its component subunits, by 'systematic' cooperation, preserve its integral configuration of structure and behavior and tend to restore it after nondestructive disturbances"[7] (i.e., disturbances of the whole as such).

3. We still have to determine the nature of behavior's relationship to this overall dynamics, and the meaning of innateness in the context of a hierarchy of systems as compared to the context of the orthodox neo-Darwinian concept of genetic determination.

On the first point, Weiss's position is unequivocal: in its initial forms behavior is innate. Motor behavior may be observed in the embryo prior to any experience of the external world, as well as in the preneural stage of motor activity.[8] The embryonic brain also manifests an activity predating any regulated function. But this innateness of the early stages should be looked upon, even more than the morphogenesis of systems, as the outcome of a "formative dynamics," bearing in mind that "most of the fundamental organismic operations are carried on decidedly *without the benefit of predesigned circuitry.*"[9] In the initial stages of the embryology of the nervous system, "pioneering fibers" find their way into areas alien to their own environment. From these non-nervous zones they get "orienting cues." Through a "towing process," the nerve is then "drawn out by the growth . . . of its terminal tissues," as fibers which have "reached their destination" show the path for others to follow.[10] In discussing this example and many others (coral colonies, etc.), Weiss lays much stress on the compatibility between "great over-all regularity and individual uniqueness" of details. He evokes the banal case of trees, the fact that an oak, a pine, or a poplar is instantly identifiable by its shape "even though each specimen is individually unique. Such standardized end forms [defy] any logical attempt to regard the product as just the blind outcome of a bunch, or call it a sum, of microprecisely programmed cause-effect sequences of linear chain reactions in the sense of a naïve mechanical machine concept."[11]

In short, the innate character of behavior in its early manifestations is a synthesis of preformations and constructions. Such early behavior is *preformed* inasmuch as it expresses the general "organization" of any living organism, thus constituting a specific manifestation of the dynamic of "systems" with its three characteristics: the relative invariability of the "whole"; its coordinating function in relation to the component parts; and its compensatory action in response to disturbances. But it is also *constructive* inasmuch as it depends neither on detailed programming nor on any straightforwardly exogenous action of the environment, and consists in an activity directed at the environment embodying a flexibility consistent with the capacity to respond to disturbance or diversity in external conditions.

This consubstantiality, as it were, between behavior and the actual organization of the system is clearly shown by a diagram of Weiss's illustrating the development of the nervous system from the genome and the ooplasm to the terminal connections, via at least forty different processes linked here by eighty directional arrows expressing their relations. What Weiss is describing is "a maze of innumerable intersecting pathways, each varying in some unpredictable degree according to the local circumstances of the moment. The demonstrable reality of [this] variability *en route* defies any attempt to fall back on a concept of machine-like microprecision as explanation of developmental order, and by the same token, makes the recourse to system theory compelling."[12] This diagram thus clearly points up the basic identity between the dynamics of the system as, so to speak, "internal behavior," and behavior in the strict sense of the dynamics of action oriented toward the environment.

4. But while it is true that behavior is innate in its origins, there are many instances, particularly once a certain degree of complexity is attained, where new varieties of behavior are generated by phenotypical accommodations before the advent of hereditary forms. This process, phenocopy, has no doubt even played an important role in evolution, as we shall see in the next chapter. This being so, the genetic mechanism of this replacement process is very difficult to explain, and, as I noted in Chapter Three, Mayr speaks of an "unknown process" in this regard. Now, while this problem is indeed impossible to resolve from a standpoint of neo-Darwinism, Weiss's conception of interlocking subsystems, and of higher systems exerting an overall dynamic action over lower ones instead of merely being made up of them, tends to simplify things considerably.

Weiss's main objection to the classical interpretation of the genome's action is that "there is neither logical nor factual support for the supposition that organization can be explained in reference to gene interactions *alone.*"[13] The logical error Weiss exposes is to argue as though the gene were able to introduce organization into "the orderless processes in its unorganized milieu, so as to mold the latter into the coordinated teamwork that is to culminate in an accomplished organism," as though the "information" or "control" emanating from the genome were unidirectional. This amounts to an *a priori* ascription of organizational capacities to the genome. But the existence of such capacities cannot be taken for granted, and to extrapolate in this way from their presence in higher systems which, in this view, the genome is supposed to generate on its own is a completely circular argument. It is true that the genes possess such properties, but they are not specific to them; and here the facts back up good logic, because wherever we are inclined to see "actions," it turns out that there is only "interaction." Admittedly, "The transfer of order from DNA through RNA to protein is comparable to the translation of *words* from one language into another. But how to get from words to the meaningful *syntax* of language?" The fact is that "genes, highly organized in themselves, do not impart higher order upon an orderless milieu by ordainment, but that they themselves are part and parcel of an ordered system, in which they are enclosed and with the patterned dynamics of which they interact. The organization of this supra-genic system, the organism . . . has ever been present since the primordial living systems, passed down in uninterrupted continuity from generation to generation through the organic matrix in which the genome is encased."[14]

Such statements, so contrary to the predominant view in genetics, suggest at first glance that, when it comes to the famous problem of the chicken and the egg, genetics prefers the egg and Weiss the chicken. But I feel that Weiss's solution is not quite so simple, and, if I may be permitted to speak in terms I have used elsewhere, I would say that he has overcome this antithesis with a synthesis by opting for the chick as the necessary intermediary which simultaneously "constructs" the adult chicken and supplies it with the germinal cells it needs to manufacture eggs. In other words, the prime biological reality for Weiss is development, even if development remains as thoroughly mysterious for him as the dynamic of systems itself.

All the same, we do know enough by now to assert, in company with Weiss, that developmental processes occur in a system "in which the genes do not 'act' as independent autonomous dictators, but with which they simply 'interact' as cooperative parts."[15] Weiss illustrates these interactions in an impressive diagram.[16] Hierarchically, we see the chromosome, the nucleus, the cytoplasm (not shown: the organelles), the tissue, the organism as unified whole, and, lastly, the environment itself, which is part of the picture by virtue of selection.

We can thus see what Weiss understands by the origin of an innate characteristic. The genesis of a trait is not simply embodied in particular genes; it consists in a process which, though it begins with these genes, also encompasses a determinate sector of the epigenesis with which the genes interact. Its trajectory thus displays a certain unity which distinguishes it from others, with which furthermore it may combine. At once genic and epigenic in character, a new variation may therefore enshrine aspects which are not preformed in the genes but which are produced by the dynamics of the genes' interactions with epigenesis. As for the innateness of specific "behavior," which necessarily consists in movements rather than morphological characteristics and differences between such characteristics, there is an even higher probability here that hereditary forms are the result of a fusion of this kind between genic action and the beginnings of epigenesis. Preneural motor activity, for instance, cannot really be explained without postulating a composite outcome of this kind. It can only occur in an embryo that has already become relatively differentiated through epigenetic syntheses. Being hereditary, it naturally presupposes a genic action of phylogenetic origin. But this action does not enshrine the motor activity as such; all it can do is bring it about, inasmuch as it remains one with its epigenetic extension. Such a unity is hardly compatible with the current notion of simple combinations of discrete elements but is readily intelligible in the context of the Weissian conception of necessary interactions.

We are far from having any detailed knowledge of such interactions, of course, and Weiss is the first to acknowledge that the spectacular advances made in biology in recent decades have taught us very little—even "nothing" (see Introduction)—about the actual mechanisms of development. But this in no way detracts from the persuasiveness of the models Weiss proposes, and his evocation of "hierarchical systems" and "interactions" between the levels of a "stratified determinism" is vital to the needs of an adequate account of behavior. Given that at every phylogenetic stage behavior consists of actions directed toward the external environment, such remarkable achievements as instincts and intelligence can only be explained in two ways (assuming that one rejects the hypothesis of the universality of chance-governed origins canalized solely by selection of the "survival" type—a hypothesis which, as I have pointed out, ultimately discredits scientific knowledge itself). The first of these explanations posits a constant prophetic capacity on the part of genomes which are supposed to foresee the adequation of their products to the most differentiated environments. The second invokes interactions between the various levels of organization. We now have to determine the possible nature of such interactions in the case of the simplest forms of behavior.

Notes to Chapter Five

1. *Naturwissenschaften* (1923), 11, p. 669.
2. *Proceedings of the American Philosophical Society,* 104, pp. 242–47.
3. "The Living System: Determinism Stratified." In Paul A. Weiss, *Within the Gates of Science and Beyond* (New York: Hafner, 1971), pp. 273–74. Reprinted from *Studium Generale* (1969), 22, pp. 361–400. Also in A. Koestler and J. R. Smythies (eds.), *Beyond Reductionism* (New York: Macmillan, 1970).
4. Weiss, "Living System," *Gates of Science,* p. 270.
5. Weiss, "The Basic Concept of Hierarchic Systems." In Weiss *et al., Hierarchically Organized Systems* (New York: Hafner, 1971), p. 38.
6. Ibid., p. 12.
7. Ibid., p. 14.
8. Weiss, *Principles of Development: A Text in Experimental Embryology* (New York: Holt, 1939), pp. 567–71.
9. Weiss, "Basic Concept," p. 22.
10. Weiss, *Dynamics of Development: Experiments and Inferences* (New York: Academic Press, 1968), p. 447.
11. Weiss, "One Plus One Does Not Equal Two" (1967). In *Gates of Science,* pp. 229–30.
12. Weiss, "Basic Concept," pp. 31–33.
13. Weiss, "Living System," p. 301.
14. Ibid., pp. 302–303.
15. Weiss, "Basic Concept," p. 39.
16. Ibid., Fig. 5, p. 40. Also in "Living System," p. 303.

SIX

Phenocopy as Mediation Between Environmental Influences and Behavioral Genic Factors

THE MOST DIFFICULT problem raised—for the non-Lamarckian at any rate—by specific hereditary behavior (or "instincts") is how to account for the fact that such behavior, which is endogenous inasmuch as it is hereditary, is nevertheless informed about the environment, even to the point of embodying a whole program of action directed toward objects or occurrences outside the organism. It was in response to this difficulty that Baldwin proposed the idea of organic selection and Waddington that of genetic assimilation. Both were seeking to bridge the gap between the environmental influences responsible for the formation of phenotypical accommodations and the genome's conservative activities and mutations. But despite the importance of the factors invoked by these authors, the solutions they offer seem to me inadequate on two counts. In the first place, a chance factor remains between the phenotypical accommodation and the subsequent genic development. In the discussion cited in Chapter Four, for instance, I quoted Waddington on my *Limnaea* to the effect that even before selection the earlier genotype contains "many genes tending to produce the modified phenotype under the influence of the suitable environmental stress." This is quite possible, to be sure, but to make it a necessary precondition of any convergence between the said phenotype and the new genotype whose genesis we have to explain is to come perilously close to the neo-Darwinian idea of the selection of random mutations. The other lacuna in these approaches, to my mind, has to do with the role of selection. Where survival is selection's only concern, the evocation of the initial phenotype is no doubt sufficient, but if selection is also to be made responsible for "bringing together" and "combining," to use Waddington's terms, then we must give some account of its working in the internal environment and show how this environment, as modified by the phenotype, becomes the framework destined to mold the variations which will eventually constitute the new genotype. Such is the process which Goldschmidt has named phenocopy. I have attempted an account of it in a short work[1] which I shall now briefly summarize.

1. The phenomena referred to as the process of phenocopy are fairly commonplace in the realm of morphological variations and have been noted occasionally in the sphere of behavior. What happens is that a new trait first manifests itself in phenotypical form and then, after a phase characterized by a blend of phenotypes and incipient genotypes, the same trait, or in any case a "copy" of it, emerges as the property of a stable genotype. There has been some question as to whether the genotype copies the phenotype or vice versa. As a parti-

san of the first view, Lorenz has sought to clarify matters
by proposing the term "genocopy" in connection with a
form of behavior in certain ducks which was at first
phenotypical and then became hereditary. But it is now
standard usage to speak of phenocopy when referring to
simple instances of a former phenotype being copied by
a subsequent genotype. On the other hand, the way in
which this mechanism is conceived naturally remains
problematic. We have already seen, in Chapter Three,
how Mayr cautiously speaks of nonhereditary forms of
behavior being "replaced," thanks to an unknown process, by "genetically controlled" forms.

I have discussed the possible ways of explaining this
"unknown process" in some detail in the earlier work
just mentioned and shall not return to that discussion
here, but it is worth mentioning the now generally accepted account offered by Ehrlich and Holm in their
book *The Process of Evolution* (1963). For Ehrlich and
Holm, phenotypes, which are ordinarily very variable,
may, given a constant and well-differentiated environment, attain a stable, standard form by means of a canalization of the epigeneses influenced by this environment.
Where this occurs, any new hereditary variations produced at the level of the genome will simply be subjected
to selection by the same environment. It is thus normal,
in view of this forced convergence, that they should resemble the preceding phenotype. As to why mutations
become irreversibly fixed, despite the fact that they may
have been produced by chance, Ehrlich and Holm appeal
to Lerner's genetic homeostasis and to coadaptation of
the genes entailing the correlative modification of several distinct factors. Equilibrium need not be achieved in

these circumstances from the initiation of the selections involved in the given environment; but, once achieved, it will ensure the establishment of a "selective plateau" precluding any reversion.

Clearly, this explanation, despite its helpful introduction of the idea of genic interaction—an idea I shall make use of in connection with the instinct and its probable combinatory processes—brings us back to reliance on the notions of chance and external selection. It is chance that accounts for the production, in an environment E, of genetic variations, and since those variations incompatible with environment E will disappear, chance must produce acceptable ones if phenocopy is to occur. On this reading, the initial phenotype has but an indirect role, in that only those genotypes which allow for the formation of this phenotype are eligible for recombination; variation is thus confined to a range narrower than that of the variations possible for the initial population (before selection). The explanation of behavioral phenocopy, however, means postulating a more direct relationship, and with this in view we shall do well to think in terms of a selection of new genic variations necessarily carried out by the internal and epigenetic environment, as modified by the phenotype so as to constitute an obligatory framework which will shape the final variations.

2. Therefore, I have proposed another possible model, the principal aim of which is to meet the need, so essential when it comes to the relationship between behavior and evolution, to explain, without falling back into Lamarckianism, how the organism manages, in its specific and instinctive forms of behavior, to obtain the information which these require in order to be accepted through adequation to the environment. An interesting point in this regard is that M. W. Wickler, one of Lorenz's followers at the Seewisen Institute, argues in a fundamental article that behavior precedes and governs the formation of organs; and that both behavior and organ formation are attributable in part to selection, but also in part to genetic assimilations and phenocopies which mimic the Lamarckian action of the environment.

Let me first make clear what function I expect the mechanism of phenocopy (as I shall here define it) to perform. In the first place, it should help us account for those specific forms of behavior which I refer to as elementary, that is to say, behavior whose simplicity suggests that it has been invented by the animal in the course of processes of learning or acquisition on the phenotypical level, and then reconstructed genetically thanks to phenocopy. Secondly, I shall attach a good deal of importance to the fact that, even in cases where a phenotype becomes stabilized in a constant and differentiated environment—a situation evoked in Ehrlich and Holm's account—it does not always give rise to a phenocopy. As an example of this I have already cited those *Limnaea ovata,* among the abyssal fauna of Lake Léman, which have remained at the phenotypical stage *(profunda* and *Yungi)* and produced no phenocopies. In the realm of behavior, instances that come to mind are human language and certain birds' songs which have to be learned anew with each generation. Thus, it is probable that intermediate categories have to be established between a non-inheritable behavior and behavior which

77

can become hereditarily fixed, just as, when we compare the various kinds of instincts, we find important differences between those which are almost completely stereotyped and those which are susceptible to more or less extensive variation from one individual to the next. Thirdly, it should be noted right away that if I attribute the formation of elementary instincts to phenocopy, I do not make the same claim for the more complex forms, which are far too sophisticated in their differentiation and systematization to have been invented by an individual animal at the phenotypical level. On the other hand, although phenocopy cannot account for such forms, I would nevertheless hypothesize that they are the outcome of combinations formally analogous to certain neuronal connections (networks, etc.) which may be thought to characterize genic interactions, as well as of complementary reinforcements. This outcome would still be based, however, on possible compounds of elementary types of behavior, so that the basic information about the environment would still be obtained, albeit indirectly, from phenocopy. Thus, there can be no question as to the importance of phenocopy and its attendant problems.

The fact remains that an explanation of complex instincts has to be sought in the modifications brought about within epigenetic syntheses by the phenotypical acquisition of new forms of behavior. Since such behavior consists of action directed at the environment, these modifications are produced by the combined effects of environmental influence and the organism's own activity. But inasmuch as the epigenetic system is characterized by a hierarchy of quite distinct levels, modifications precipitated by the environment will plainly differ widely in character depending upon the level affected. The changes may involve only the higher planes, for instance, operating at the level of organs and in some cases giving rise to no significant conflicts with the hereditary programming of the species. In such circumstances there is no reason at all for the production of a phenocopy, and the phenotypical behavior will simply be reconstructed with each new generation. On the other hand, where the changes brought about by the new behavior work at a more primitive level, a disequilibrium will be set up between epigenetic innovations and genetic programming. And it is this disequilibrium that will be productive.

But what is the nature and mechanism of this process? Two hypotheses must be clearly distinguished here. One posits a direct action exerted by the modifications wrought by the change in behavior, an action working down to the genome from the higher levels of the epigenetic system. This account amounts to a reassertion of the Lamarckian action of the environment upon genetic processes. The second hypothesis is that the disequilibrium as such, along with the selections this entails, constitutes the causal factor—a very different idea. I cannot accept the first hypothesis, for reasons which almost all authors now acknowledge (despite the operation of Temin's "inverse transcriptase" between RNA and DNA —a question to which I shall come back in Chapter Seven, #11). On the other hand, I find the second hypothesis persuasive, for it is in the nature of any disequilibrium that its effects will spread so long as the initial disruptive factor has not been compensated for.

I would therefore propose the following account.

Where the disequilibrium is far-reaching, it eventually makes itself felt at the level of the regulatory genes, or at that of the genome's overall regulatory mechanisms. But what is involved here is not a coded message indicating what is occurring, nor even less one indicating what is to be done. The only message implicit here is that "something is not functioning normally." Paul A. Weiss's perspicacious observations on the fact that genes do not act "fully autonomously," but rather that they "interact" and "react" on contact with systems which are themselves organized, should have had enough impact by now for there to be nothing shocking about the idea that in the event of conflict or disequilibrium between modifications of epigenesis and the syntheses programmed by the genes, the genes may be expected to suffer the effects of the disequilibrium through a simple retroactive process of contamination—but a process, I repeat, in no way involving a codable "message" like the messages which govern synthesis.

Granted this much, I would further argue that the genome's reaction here is to try out variations. These are semi-random owing to the genome's lack of information, but they are very likely canalized toward the areas of disequilibrium; if so, total randomness is ruled out, and the idea of "trials" is more appropriate for describing what happens. It is at this point that selection carried out by an environment comes into play, but in such circumstances the environment in question must initially, and essentially, be the internal and epigenetic one. Now, this internal environment has clearly been somewhat modified by a new form of behavior that has precipitated the entire process and, thus, by extension, by the influences of the external environment which this behavior inevitably embodies. But inasmuch as the internal environment is endowed with homeostatic mechanisms, and inasmuch as the epigenetic system itself is specifically organized according to an "epigenetic homeostasis" (not to mention Waddington's "homeorhesis" with its "chreods"), the disequilibrium triggered by the new behavior is already attenuated and conflict confined to the opposition between genic variations and internal environments which have suffered modification but which are now becoming re-equilibrated. Next, and as a consequence, comes a series of selections, for the new genic variations can only become stabilized by submitting to the requirements of the modified internal environments. This necessity for the genic variations to fit in with a framework which selects them but which is itself the outcome of the modifications provoked by the new behavior, or in a general way by a new phenotype, now inevitably entails a convergence between the new genic form and the characteristics of the phenotypical behavior responsible for the changes. Clearly, then, phenocopy so understood is in no sense a hereditary "fixation" of the phenotype, but instead a replacement of the phenotype by an endogenous reconstruction implying no direct influence of the Lamarckian kind. But the convergence effected in this way results only indirectly from selections carried out by the external environment, Ehrlich and Holm's desire for a simple solution notwithstanding. It is the epigenetic environment with its specific homeostasis which is responsible for the similarities seen in phenocopy, for it is this environment which imposes itself as a framework or matrix upon the genic variations thrown up as the result of the initial disequilibrium.

Phenocopy's indispensable role, therefore, is to supply hereditary forms of behavior with the information about the external environment which they must have if they are to function. Since the genome cannot receive such information directly, this is assimilated phenotypically during epigenesis, the mechanisms of which are designed to reconcile the requirements of the genetic program with the requirements of the environment. When this environment changes and new forms of behavior exploit this change (whether or not they have provoked it), the epigenetic system is modified in consequence, becoming a new selective framework, an obligatory mold for the genic variations precipitated by this development as a whole. The new variations so selected and adapted to the structure of the modified epigenesis now converge with the initial phenotypical modification, and it is this phenocopy which, though resulting from a purely endogenous reconstruction (albeit selected by the epigenetic environment), mirrors the properties of the new environment in as much detail as if direct influence had indeed occurred.

Lastly, let me draw attention to the degree to which the above account of things simplifies the problem of the formation of instincts, no matter how unexplained these may remain in their concrete manifestations. The chief reason for this relative clarification is that if behavior, as action upon the environment, can only come into being at the higher epigenetic levels, the part played at this point by the modified epigenetic system in the canalization of genic variations will result—though by virtue of intraselection and endo-adaptation—in these variations being supplied with the same information and orientation they would receive if direct environmental determination existed. But the great advantage to the idea of an intimate formative collaboration between the genome and an epigenesis which it governs but upon which it also depends, as compared with the Lamarckian notion of simple external action or the Darwinian one of external selection, lies in the fact that the entire process depends on the necessity for endogenous reconstructions. Perhaps this can help us dispel some of the mystery from the different aspects of the genesis of instincts, a genesis which despite being endogenous displays an astounding conformity with even the least evident properties of the environment.

Notes to Chapter Six

1. Jean Piaget, *Adaptation vitale et psychologie de l'intelligence. Sélection organique et phénocopie* (Paris: Hermann, 1975).
2. M.W. Wickler, "Vergleigende Verhaltensforschung und Phylogenetik." In G. Heborer, *Die Evolution der Organismen* (1967), 1, p. 461.

SEVEN

Psychobiological Speculations on the Problems of Instincts in Relation to the Problems of Evolution

INSTINCTS ARE SCARCELY ever treated as entities nowadays, for we now have a better idea of the extreme complexity of instinctual mechanisms. We also realize how difficult it is to disentangle the respective roles of innate factors and acquired variations (or, in other words, of maturational and experiential components) when considering any given form of behavior broadly described as instinctive. I shall therefore adopt Hinde's reserved position, which characterizes as instinctive those activities peculiar to a species, so implying some relationship with innateness but making no advance assumptions as to the nature of this relationship.[1]

1. As for the problem of the origin of instincts, even understood in this broad sense of species-specific activity, everyone is now extremely reluctant to tackle it, so lacking are we in even the most elementary experimental data relating to the nature of an instinct *in statu nascendi*. However, I am rash enough to feel that, even if this

problem is as hard to solve today as it was in earlier centuries, it is still essential that we discuss it and examine all feasible hypotheses regarding its solution. Although instincts are inseparably linked to the physiological organization of living things of all levels of complexity, any attempt to couch accounts of their genesis in the language of modern biology produces formulations extremely paradoxical from the genetic point of view. For example, let us take a case where a specific (even multispecific) form of behavior, the crawling of slowworms and snakes, with the many anatomical modifications which locomotion of this kind calls for (general lengthening of the body and organs, along with the nervous and muscular development prerequisite to undulation), becomes necessary in order to compensate for the unfavorable if not dangerous effects of a hereditary variation of a negative kind such as the loss of limbs. It is an untenable claim that in ophidians and slowworms crawling preceded apodia, and that their members, though present initially, atrophied or became susceptible to various diseases because they were not used. In the case of the slowworm, we may even observe some of the earlier stages of the subtractive variation involved. The progression is from lizards to skinks with four little tridactylous limbs limited in their use, to the *Ophisausus apodus,* which has only hind members, actually little more than stumps, and thus to the slowworm itself. Variations of a negative kind[2] have indeed taken place, therefore, and crawling in its different forms (undulation, rectilinear progression, and a variety of other complex movements) in different (terrestrial, arboreal, aquatic) environments thus

constitutes a compensation. We can even see the beginnings of this development in the Mediterranean lizard
Seps, which has very short limbs, which it uses for moving
slowly but which it folds back along its body when it has
to move more quickly and adopt an undulatory crawl.
One might, of course, assign one cause to crawling and
apodia alike, and Grassé proposes as just such a common
cause a general lengthening of the skeleton (an increase
in the number of presacral vertebrae). But if such a
lengthening is the cause and not the outcome of crawling, what is the reason for it? And why has it not led to
a correlative development of the limbs, as in the alliga-
tor, with its five-meter length? In any case, even granted
such a common cause, the essential fact I want to stress
remains: there is a necessity for a new form of behavior
capable of playing a compensatory role in regard to a
negative variation liable to have adverse effects.

The problem here—a central one when it comes to the
formation of instinctive behavior—is, of course, to decide whether the same genetic mechanism is responsible,
on the one hand, for those random variations the degree
of whose acceptability or nonacceptability to the environment is only established by *ex post facto* selections,
and, on the other hand, for kinds of behavior presupposing the application to the environment of a certain savoir-faire—and also, in this particular case, playing a
compensatory role in relation to a subtractive variation.
Two solutions come to mind, and indeed at first glance
they seem to be the only possible ones. The first is that
the compensation has been achieved thanks to individual
initiatives, i.e., on the level of phenotypical *accommodats,*
and that these have subsequently been replaced by a

genic entity of the phenocopy type. The second possibility is that the subtractive variation and the compensatory behavior are both hereditary from the start. But this account clearly makes things very complicated. For one thing, it makes the genetic mechanism responsible for a variation which threatens the species. For another, it means that this mechanism corrects itself by means, not just of anatomical variations, but also of a program of coordinated movements enabling an animal which has reached a certain stage of its epigenesis to behave adequately on land, in the water, or in the trees. One cannot object in principle to the suggestion that a succession of random occurrences will eventually produce compensatory effects. But just how long will this take—and how many unsuccessful effects will have to be produced first? At the same time, while it is clear that sexual recombinations, affecting already selected traits, limit variations and thus produce a stable selective plateau, such recombinations remain random in their associations. Generally speaking, since all behavior is teleonomic inasmuch as it is action directed toward the external environment, it is hard to see how this goal-directedness, which is in evidence from the outset, can be reconciled with a chance-governed genesis, except perhaps to the extent that an element of chance may be said to operate within a trial-and-error procedure which is, for its part, subject to overall orientation. Determination by chance is even less plausible where compensation occurs. Further, selection of the "survival" type (in the absolute sense of the differential rate of reproduction, etc.) does not constitute a sufficient explanation of adequation. The question that has to be answered, therefore, is whether, where certain elementary forms have successfully become fixed through phenocopy, presupposing the establishment of new connections between the genome and epigenesis, a combinatorial system embodying these new connections can give rise to a nonrandom structure made up of coherent subsystems (networks, etc.) appropriate to the operation of implicational relationships, compensatory mechanisms, etc., which can determine *ex ante facto* as well as *ex post facto* the entire range of possibilities opened up by the initial phenocopies.

2. Let me now state the aims of the present chapter, which are three. The first, naturally, is to try and distinguish between the "possible" hypotheses concerning the formation of instincts. Among such possible hypotheses I would include even those which cannot at present be tested but which for viable theoretical reasons deserve to be treated as more or less plausible.

The second aim is, given a merely plausible hypothesis, to try and ascertain the necessary and sufficient conditions for the operation of the mechanism it postulates. As for compensatory processes, taken here as an example, we are familiar with all kinds of these on the epigenetic level, in the functioning of the nervous system, and so on. We are also familiar with genetic homeostasis, and a process of regulation of mutations has been hypothesized. But the question is whether such models can cope with the supposed formation of compensatory behavior engendered by hereditary variations which are the outcome of genic combinations—or whether the necessary conditions are so many and varied that we cannot in every instance avoid admitting defeat and appealing to an all-powerful "chance." These are the kinds of questions I think worth asking.

My third aim is in a way a synthesis, or at any rate a condensation, of the first two, a detailed treatment of which would require a book in itself. I shall try to simplify things by identifying the mechanisms common to all types of behavior where a part is played by the thing which constitutes and remains the chief mystery of instincts—namely, an anticipation of future situations which is intimately dependent on the environment and on possible changes in it. What we find here, in fact, is a differentiated and detailed savoir-faire which, if accounted for in terms of representational intelligence, presupposes a level of inferential capacity and of systematic coordination far higher—and often far more wide-scale—than that of the animal's abilities as displayed when it is confronted experimentally with tasks alien to its specific instinctual programming. How, in such cases, is harmony achieved between the organism's behavior and external objects or occurrences? The fact that we can scarcely begin to answer this question does not mean that we should not try to discern certain common processes. If we succeed, the problem of formation will naturally arise, and this under two aspects whose complementarity may be very instructive. For, on the one hand, being general in nature, these processes may turn out to have a formative role in regard to particular instincts; on the other hand, again because of their generality, their own formation may have to be sought within that global organizational dynamics whose importance has been constantly underlined by Paul A. Weiss, who also stresses, however, our serious lack of information in this area.

In the absence of such knowledge, we can offer no more than an overall description of the supposed processes, making no attempt—except in the first two cases —to trace their geneses. Needless to say, this question remains an open one. The processes in question must not be assumed to be involved in invariable form in any given organization, and we should bear in mind that they are themselves subject to the mechanisms of evolution.

3. I shall distinguish seven main processes in this connection, taking them in order of increasing complexity. The simplest—and probably the most general, for it occurs in the plant world (see Chapter Eight)—is the shift from a regular succession $A/B/C$ to a goal-directed anticipation where the attainment of C implies a prior search for or effectuation of A and B. An example of this is sleep, which at first has a restorative function in relation to the intoxications which provoke it, but which then becomes an anticipatory precaution against such excessive fatigue. In this instance we are already dealing with a form of behavior; but, as a matter of fact, any physiological feedback can itself effect the transition from a repeated sequence to anticipations associated with corrective measures. A second essential process will develop sooner or later out of this first one. This is generalization, where a form of specific behavior is used for new purposes in a new situation. Sleep may serve as an example here too, in that it becomes part of the hibernation instincts, protecting the animal from undernourishment and no longer just from intoxication. When a type of behavior calls for the coordination of several factors, a third general process comes into play, constituted by the combinatorial system that links these elements up in the various ways possible. This process explains the very common phenomenon of multiple behavioral variations found among closely related species even though this variability cannot be explained either by selection or by the demands of the environment. This combinatorial system, which I describe as "extrinsic," is extended by a fourth, more complex, "intrinsic" process embodying differentiations and integrations between distinct sub-systems. In addition, a fifth process brings compensatory mechanisms into the picture. In processes one through four, a part is of course played by regulations as corrective or reinforcing factors, but their role is that of the mechanisms inherent in all vital organization. It may happen, by contrast, that the principal motor of particular behavior is the necessity to annul or compensate for an endogenous disturbance, and this is where our fifth process comes in. This formative process is illustrated in the animal world by the case of crawling discussed earlier, and among plants by the reinforcement of chlorophyll and of the capacity for photosynthesis when a species finds itself in unfavorable circumstances (see Chapter Eight). The two processes I have yet to mention are still very mysterious, although there can be no doubt as to their actual existence. They operate in cases where the regulatory action is not confined to compensation but tends to fill gaps by supplying a complementary formation, the novelty of which creates very serious problems. I thus use the term "complementary reinforcements" (process six) to denote the phylogenetically progressive formation of certain organs intimately bound up with behavior, such as legs; and I speak of "constructive coordinations" where such developments further require detailed information on the environment, as, for instance, with the production of stinging organs and of toxic substances in the case of the coelenterate nematocyst (cf. also, for that matter, nettles and many other plants).

Now, when one considers these seven classes of processes, all more or less general and formative of countless hereditary forms of behavior, one cannot fail to be struck by their functional convergence with the mechanisms of intelligence itself: anticipations, generalizations, combinatorial systems, compensations, and complementary constructions generating new structures—all do indeed correspond to the basic procedures of human intelligence, so that at first glance one might be tempted to follow Cuénot and endow every genome with a "combinatorial intelligence" which produces "tools." But such a reading is quite mistaken and must be rejected on the following clear grounds. What is connoted by the dangerous term "intelligence" ("dangerous" because ever liable to suggest that what is involved is a "faculty") is a set of coordinating mechanisms which allow the individual subject to discover new problems and to organize, with a view to their solution, sequences of specific operations. These operations certainly include the various types of processes I have just enumerated. But the uniqueness of intelligence lies in free compositions of a variety and specificity always subject to revision in function of a constant constructive activity. For it is the individual himself who is subjected to his problems, who chooses or invents them, whereas the elementary processes we call anticipations, generalizations, combinations, etc., cannot be categorized as intelligence because they are not intentionally organized and used by an individual subject with a specific, new solution in view. That such intelligent acts are possible and even frequent beyond the realm of instincts, and even at certain fairly primitive phylogenetic levels, is now firmly established, but this in no way justifies applying the epithet "intelligent" to specific forms of behavior with a fixed hereditary core covering both the posing of the problem concerned and its solution, on the sole grounds that such behavior already involves such very general organic mechanisms as the seven elementary processes I have distinguished. In short, the generality of these processes certainly proves that intelligence is rooted in the life of the organism (as I argued in *Biology and Knowledge*), but this is no reason to conflate intelligence and instinct. Perhaps an analogy will serve to explain the distinction I draw between instincts and intelligence. Well in advance of the emergence of a brain, some lower animals such as the *Coelenterata* display many functional characteristics which at a higher stage the brain will develop, coordinate, and centralize. These include perceptual sensitivity, motor commands, learning capacity, etc. Now, the fact that such processes exist long before the constitution of a brain obviously does not mean that we have to postulate the existence at this point of an invisible centralizing organ responsible for their effective operation. Similarly, the existence within the instinctual realm of elementary mechanisms which intelligence will

94

later freely coordinate gives us no call whatsoever to deem intelligence responsible for such already present general processes.

4. The thesis I want to put forward regarding the genesis of hereditary behavior (i.e., activities characteristic of a species or group of species, taxonomically speaking) may be broken down into three complementary hypotheses. The first posits the existence of what I call "elementary" varieties of behavior. The specificity of such behavior is that it occurs at a level attainable by somatic pathways or, in other words, through phenotypical *accommodats.* I would qualify such behavior as elementary even in those cases where, on the level on which we observe it, it belongs to the genotypical inheritance of the species, so long as we have good reason to consider this level simple enough (in other situations) to be an individual acquisition. The second hypothesis is that when such elementary behavior manifests itself as hereditary, it has been produced through phenocopy, the mechanism of which I described in detail in Chapter Six. There are two reasons for thinking this. In the first place, since all behavior consists of action directed toward the environment, we have to choose between a fortuitous origin and a series of trials effected through contact with external conditions, at an initial level which is already somatic. Secondly, the selection process governing success here is not simply a matter of survival but involves adequation, whence comes the primordial role of the internal environment as modified by phenotypical accommodations. Since genetic reconstruction through phenocopy is only possible where these two preconditions are met, it is the mechanism most likely to be responsible for the formation of elementary hereditary behavior. Hence my third hypothesis, namely, that complex specific behavior—i.e., behavior occurring at a level higher than that at which acquisitions through phenocopy are possible—is the product of those combinatorial, compensatory, and constructive mechanisms which exist, as I have argued, in addition to the anticipatory and generalizing capacities already operative at the elementary levels. That such mechanisms exist, and that they can play a part in genetic combinations and recombinations, is a view supported by the nature of the structure of the nervous system itself, whose dependence on the genome is beyond doubt. For as McCullogh has shown in a well-known contribution, the connections between neuronal actions (and hence dynamic as opposed to anatomical connections) are isomorphic with a Boolean network or, in other words, with a combinatorial system with all its attendant internal compensatory mechanisms and its ramifications. If the most important hereditary organ in the organization of behavior is structured in this way, there is no reason why the genes responsible for the genetic reconstruction of elementary behavior should not combine among themselves according to the available possibilities, so generating something very different from chance mutations in that the outcome is syntheses structured like networks, or perhaps other composite forms, but in any case forms that are systematic and not random.

Let us now consider in turn each of the seven general processes I have postulated and see what possibilities they open up for deductive explanatory models.

• • •

5. To begin with specific elementary behavior, but with forms where the fact of succession promotes anticipation and possible generalizations, an especially instructive instance is the "pseudopodia" of the *Amoebae.* If one wishes (in the absence, at least until now, of any precise laboratory method in this sphere) to get a picture of the way in which an "instinct" is formed, it would seem that the stages of this process may in this particular instance be inferred without too great a risk of error. As an expression of the need for nourishment, behavior proper begins here as soon as the organism establishes a relationship with the food outside, which has to be ingested through the cell wall. This relationship is subject to variation, and this variation is what triggers the actions which the animal exerts upon the outside world and which by definition constitute behavior's starting point. The simplest form of behavior in this context consists in the immediate absorption of food on chance contact with it; even here, however, a choice must be made between food and alien objects to be ignored or even avoided. Further differentiation must be assumed to occur where instead of depending on direct contact the organism can become aware of the presence of food a short distance away (through water movement), or where the cell's flexible casing forms protrusions prefiguring the later pseudopodia. Before pseudopodia proper can appear, two more important and closely associated differentiations are called for. In the first place, the animal begins actively looking for food instead of relying on chance encounters. Secondly, and as a corollary, the repeated succession of events regularly corresponding to

97

the animal's actions engenders a capacity for anticipation which endows its searching with a purpose and an implicit expectation of success. The pseudopodia themselves constitute systematic formations inasmuch as they are food-gathering implements, and hence organs created by behavior, but at the same time they are no more than temporary organelles in that they are retracted after use to be replaced by others which will form when the need arises.

But no matter how simple the formation of pseudopodia through somatic or phenotypical initiatives may seem, the fact remains that what we are dealing with is a specific form of behavior—behavior, therefore, which is hereditarily fixed in its basic pattern, even though individual variations of detail are naturally possible on the level of accommodations. With regard to this process of genic construction or reconstruction, while it is easy to accept that the genome must embody complete information on the internal organization of the unicellular amoeba for whose epigenesis it is responsible, it is very hard to imagine by what mechanisms it could be informed on the movements and actions which this organism will have to carry out in order to reach external food (even assuming that the nature of these food sources is predetermined). For, I repeat, behavior consists in actions exerted upon an environment which transcends the somatic realm and presupposes goals over and above those of the biochemical programming of morphogenesis. The only two possible solutions are thus chance-plus-external-selection, and phenocopy-plus-selection-effected-by-the-internal-environment. But in the case of a development as simple as the one we have just been discussing, and particularly in view of such a direct and unwavering teleonomy, the appeal to chance is little more than an empty verbal convention.

A final point in this connection is that while pseudo-podia supply us with a good instance of the transition from succession to anticipation, they are also susceptible of *generalization* to the extent that they contribute to loco-motion, to displacements of the entire organism. It is possible, in fact, that an analogous formative mechanism involving phenocopy was behind the development of those permanent extensions of the *flagellum* type found in *Mastigamoeba*.

6. The process leading from succession to anticipa-tion is often clearly manifested in phenotypical accom-modations. By contrast, the process I am calling general-ization can only be inferred, and then only with some difficulty, especially when our basis is comparisons on the phylogenetic level. All the same, a comparative ap-proach of this kind presents a great deal of interest for our purposes, for if under the rubric of generalization we include not only changes in the functional significance of behavior but also the mechanism whereby new behavior makes use of an already existing organ while at the same time radically modifying its external functions, we are confronted by a formative mode very hard to ascribe simply to mutations. It should be remembered that while it has been possible to bring about a great number of hitherto unknown mutations in the laboratory, no one has yet managed to create a new instinct under such conditions—a very instructive fact in itself. In cases where generalization consists in the linking of nonprede-

termined behavior to organs developed long before for quite other purposes—and this without modifying morphogenesis—the type of refinement involved seems an especially far cry from a process of production by means of random mutations in that all that occurs is a fresh utilization of what already exists.

A striking example here is the alimentary behavior of lamellibranchiates, molluscs which have ended up using their lamellate branchiae as a filter for retaining organic matter in suspension in the water. Thus, according to Martin Wells,[3] American oysters of the genus *Crassostrea* pump between thirty and forty liters per hour through branchiae which no longer have a respiratory function, and retain only two to four milligrams of solid matter, of which only a fraction, after sorting by means of a mucus, actually serves as food. Such behavior is unquestionably linked with the sedentary life of these animals, which since they do not go in search of food are obliged by some means or another to collect it on the spot. But the interesting thing about the procedure they have adopted is that, aside from the production of mucus (which is easy for molluscs), nothing is involved here except substitution and compensation. The respiratory function of the branchiae is abandoned and the task transferred to the entire body surface, while the branchial lamellae are pressed into the service of a filtering process governed by criteria of kind, size, etc. (*Crassostrea virginica* even eliminates certain bacteria from what it accepts as food.) There can clearly be nothing random about such a system of substitution and compensation. There are only two possible conclusions, therefore. The first is that the system begins with a trial-and-error experimentation on the part of the adult animal (or on the part of an animal having reached the necessary level of ontogenetic development), and that eventually these phenotypical accommodations are replaced by endogenous phenocopies. Alternatively, it might be argued that the system is generated directly through genic combinations. If so, however, it is clear that no chance mutations are involved, and that the actual mechanism of these combinations embodies the information necessary to ensure the future changes of function. For example, it would be consistent with this account to say that the genes responsible for a form of nutrition based on an osmosis operating solely through the integument had changed places, so to speak, with those hitherto governing a branchial respiration, and so on. But, whichever of the two solutions is adopted, the fact is that the alimentary behavior of these animals displays a capacity for generalization in that a transition is made from a more primitive to a more systematic functioning.

Generalizations may also be simpler in form; indeed they may be found at every level of complexity. The crudest are those where a procedure which has worked for one instinct is simply used in the operation of another, or else where the same procedure is used from the outset for both instincts, so that a single method is immediately generalized precisely because of its simplicity. Thus, woodpeckers, endowed with an unusually powerful and rapid beak-action designed to let them catch worms embedded in tree trunks, use the same technique for carving out their nests. It is tempting, perhaps, to attribute this generalization to the selective advantages of protection, but we must not forget how often woodpeckers' nests are pillaged by starlings. Similarly, as I have noted elsewhere, the breeding places of terrestrial molluscs, which are shallow hollows in the ground, are doubtless quite unrelated to these same animals' self-protective behavior when they bury themselves in the earth in response to drought or, more typically, in hibernation. Generalizations as simple as these may of course be the outcome of phenotypical behavior followed by phenocopy. Others are more complex, like those which I believe are intrinsic to what Tinbergen and Lorenz have called derived or displaced activities. The search for the common phylogenetic origin of forms of behavior which are now differentiated has in fact turned up changes of function, known as ritualizations, which invest social signals with new meanings. Lorenz has shown, for example, in connection with provocative behavior in ducks (i.e., females) of the *Anatinae,* that the further such behavior gets "from its original menacing purpose, and the more it rigidifies in a new motor coordination of a completely fixed kind, the more it assumes the role of a signal with a new meaning."[4] Thus, once threatening behavior on the part of the female mallard directed toward a rival for her mate is transformed into "signs of love" directed at the mate himself.

In such cases, as in that of the mechanics of feeding in oysters, the generalization leads from a simpler initial state to a more complex final one, with the initial state disappearing in the process. Therefore, these cases have to be distinguished from generalizations where behavioral patterns come to be shared by two or more instinctive activities in a complementary way, without supersession. But two important points have to be emphasized.

The first is that we are not dealing here with intelligent acts as defined in #3 above. These processes are much more primitive than that; they remain organic even though they are destined much later to be incorporated and perfected by intelligence. The second point is that the link between the initial behavior and the eventual form is nevertheless generalizing in its actual meaning. The first implies the second in some sense; the desire to chase away a rival implies an affective bond with the male, and this bond is itself the basis of the generalization. This blend of, as it were, extensional transfers and quasi-implicational connections between meanings is not restricted to the process of generalization, and we shall come upon it again in dealing with combinatorial systems.

7. The difficult problems arise when we turn our attention to combinatorial systems, for it is on these that we depend—at least initially—for an explanation of the transition from elementary instincts, whose genesis may be the result of phenocopy, to complex instincts, which in varying degree transcend everything that can conceivably be ascribed to individual phenotypical initiative. My hypothesis is that, once a certain number of elementary hereditary behavioral forms have been acquired, the genic connections on which they rest tend—though naturally at various speeds implying very different time-spans—to actualize all the possible combinations compatible with the initial elements. Two sets of data make this hypothesis relatively plausible. The first comes from the inorganic world, where, in systems embodying a total number of possible intrinsic variations, all of these tend

to be realized. In the structure of a crystal, for instance, thirty-two groupings and more than two hundred sub-groupings, both cyclical and hexagonal, are possible, and every one occurs in nature. The same is true for chemical combinatorial systems, etc. Secondly, it is now generally agreed that genes do not operate in isolated fashion but in various combinations, witness the morphological variations due to the recombinations occasioned by sexual reproduction. In the case of behavior, the elements to be combined are actions, and a combinatorial system of actions, in the form of a "unified whole," constitutes a "logic." Thus, two actions may be combined or disassociated, implicationally linked or incompatible, and so on. McCullogh and Pitts have demonstrated the existence of such a case in the relations between neuronal actions, and there is no reason to suppose that something similar does not happen if the genes responsible for two or more elementary forms of behavior combine. Needless to say, a genic combinatorial system of this kind does not have to be governed by an intelligence or by a subject. On the contrary, it is precisely where the complex combinations displayed by an instinct could *not* have been invented or discovered by the animal in its somatic or phenotypical activity that we are obliged to invoke an endogenous combinatorial system coming about of necessity as a function of the possible "coadaptations" between genes, in a way analogous to what happens in a physical or neuronic system like those just mentioned. Now, to the extent that the genome cannot be reduced to a mass of arbitrarily thrown-together autonomous particles—to the extent, in other words, that it constitutes instead a system of interactions—the unified whole that it tends to actualize in its structure itself embodies an interplay of differentiations and integrations which generate consistent innovations. Therefore, this implicit logic of the genome, which might be compared to a combinatorial machine, is the only reasonable place to seek an explanation of the growing complexity of so many instincts, always assuming, of course, that enough elementary forms of behavior exist at the outset to supply this sytem with the necessary components.

Support for this account would seem to come from two sources. First, there is the existence of multiple variations among neighboring species. The proliferation of such variations raises problems having to do with what might be called an extrinsic combinatorial system (the third of our seven processes). The second source of confirmation has to do, on the contrary, with an intrinsic combinatorial system (our fourth process) involving differentiation of parts and coordination between them according to a variety of relationships, some reminiscent of meaningful implication (in the sense of comprehension), some of exclusion, and so on.

As far as extrinsic combinatorial systems are concerned, it is worth mentioning the interesting contributions of Hall (1962) and Thielcke (1964) on the songs of birds of closely related species. These songs consist of common elements (unvarying short sequences) combined in different ways, but it is not clear whether this outcome results from a pre-existing combinatorial system or merely from recombinations. On the other hand, Alexander's work (1962) on the chirping of crickets, an area also explored by Wickler,[5] points up what is rather clearly a process of combination through differentiation. This process is traced both by cross-studying subfamilies and by observing the internal development of particular subfamilies, with partial parallelisms being found between evolutionary sequences.

One of the best examples of an extrinsic combinatorial system is spiders' webs. These give the impression that the goal of each species has been to invent its own particular form, from the simplest to the most elaborate. Among the more complex webs, that of *Latrodectus pallida* has three parts: a lateral retreat complete with chamber and corridor; a ten-to-fifteen-centimeter bridge; and a complicated trapping web. The whole thing takes several days to spin and undergoes constant refinement after completion. There are two points to note here. In the first place, no one has been able to discover any adaptive or selective advantage of one type of web over another, and Le Guelte showed in 1967 that spiders can catch flies almost as easily in other kinds of webs as in their own. The only functional reason he was able to advance regarding the diversity of webs was that it perhaps facilitated sexual identification within species, but it will be readily conceded that such ingenious creatures might be expected to devise a less extravagant method of recognizing their sexual partners. Secondly—and to my mind even more instructively—no one has managed to establish any phyletic line of descent in this connection, and Witt[6] is of the opinion that no type of web can be said to derive from any other. The only ontogenetic evidence to emerge is the fact that adult *Zygiella* construct webs with a free sector which they cross by means of a single thread, whereas the young spiders produce a web with no such gap (as do the adults of other species). When young *Zygiella* are prevented from spinning, however, they immediately reproduce the species-specific web, complete with gap, on reaching adulthood. Consequently, Witt doubts that common characteristics in different types of webs point to a common origin, and he treats such cases as the simple outcome of adaptive convergences.

In a case such as this, which has been given such close attention, the formation of specific behavior certainly seems to imply the intervention of a combinatorial mechanism. The starting point must of course be at least two elementary forms of behavior: the direct pursuit of the prey prior to any spinning, then the production of a single thread enabling the spider to travel through the air from a higher position in order to reach a fly below. This utilization of a single thread might be likened to the constitution of a temporary pseudopodium. But once the possibility of permanent, stable, and interconnected threads opens up, the genes responsible can combine among themselves according to the various patterns realizable. In this way, the results obtainable by means of on-the-spot adjustments in actual actions through phenotypical initiatives and phenocopy are transcended in greater or lesser degree. This is not to say that such individual accommodations no longer occur: Witt cites the case of two individuals whose places were changed in the early stages of spinning and who proceeded to work "mirror-fashion," and that of an abnormal individual leaving open one or more spirals of its web, with variations observed over a month. Attention has also been drawn to the effect of limitations on size and of the nature of the frame available. But individual differences of this kind account for only very slight divergences from the specific programming, and it seems incontestable that the diversity of webs must be explained by a genic combinatorial system governing the various arrangements made possible by a unified whole, of which the components are geometric forms.

This hypothesis is less tautological, and also less straightforward, than it might seem at first glance, for an ensemble of variations may answer to two very different kinds of causality in genic functioning. Variations may result from the modification of particular genes—i.e., from mutations in the strict sense. But they may also be the outcome of new links between genes which remain unmodified but which have hitherto had no direct relationship. This happens even in the familiar "recombinations" of sexual reproduction. As far as instincts are concerned, this distinction is most important. "Mutations" in themselves are fortuitous, and affinities between their results need betoken no more than the effect of *a posteriori* selections. A "combinatorial system," by contrast, will give rise to genuinely related variations: the combinations *AB, AC, BC,* etc., will have links by virtue of their common components, but also differences which are the source of innovation. It is precisely this two-sided nature of such systems which to my mind supplies the necessary precondition for the transition from elementary behavior to complex instincts, for if we are going to say that these instincts possess creativity and an internal logic yet cannot be governed by an intelligence, we must ascribe these apparently superior qualities to a physical combinatorial system the postulation of which implies no more anthropomorphism than explaining the variety of crystals in terms of thirty-two "groups" of transformations. Of course, we shall still have to explain what logical links govern such genic combination—a question which arises in connection with our fourth process, intrinsic combination.

But before coming to that process, I want to mention the multiple beak variations observed by Darwin in finches of the Galápagos Islands and in Hawaiian *Drepaniidae.* The diversity of form here, in contrast to that of spiders' webs, has a functional justification. Darwin's explanation appeals on the one hand to competition, which obliges each species to specialize in respect of its ecological niche and its food sources, and on the other hand to selections, in that the change of niche leads to a change in the form of the beak by way of a choice between the variations available. A point on which Darwin is quite clear is that these available variations constitute a pre-existing, unoriented diversity and that the selection process operates upon the elements present—on what we should now call a set of mutations—until the organ itself becomes specialized, and competition for the means of existence is thus overcome. There is no need for me to emphasize how inspired Darwin's now classical account was at the time he put it forward, or to insist on the importance of the universally accepted and indispensable notion of selection. His interpretation nevertheless leaves a nagging doubt in the mind, one which he must have eventually felt himself, because in his last edition of *The Origin of Species* he added Lamarck's hereditary acquired characteristics to the factors he had already adduced, without being aware, of course, of the negative empirical evidence which has since emerged in this regard. His motive for recognizing the Lamarckian factor was, inevitably, the need to simplify the relationship between changes in behavior and changes in correlated organs. For Darwin's initial version may be interpreted in two ways. The first, which increases the role of chance, is the path that leads to the well-known excesses of a neo-Darwinism based solely on mutationism and the genetics of populations. The second places more emphasis on the activity of the organism itself, but this view has tended to remain implicit rather than explicit. In the first perspective, it is contingent circumstances that subject the animal to ever more intense competition; it is thanks to sheer good fortune that it finds unexploited ecological niches in the environment; and, above all, it must wait for favorable mutations to be thrown up by chance. Individuals unblessed by such gifts of fate will be eliminated, and only bearers of mutations enabling them to peck up grain or insects, say, can expect to be retained by the selection process. The great lacuna in explanations of this kind (aside, of course, from the increasing improbability of conjunction between n appropriate yet independent chance factors) is clearly the absence of any relationship between those genes, modifiable solely by mutations, which determine the form of organs and those equally mutable ones which are responsible for the heredity of behavior. How is it that these mutations always converge if they are chance-governed? And to what hecatombs must the hordes of the ill-adapted be condemned so as to ensure the survival of the happy few? Darwin himself had little to do with such neo-Darwinian paradoxes. He never envisaged a selection process operating on a body of successively generated chance mutations. Rather, he saw this process as a choice between simultaneously available variations—a very different conception and one which is consistent with the idea that the inheritance of types of behavior on the one hand, and modified organs on the other, are the outcome of combinations between genes and not of mutations either of individual genes or of several genes at once—which would make this inheritance incomprehensible.

An interesting case, bridging extrinsic and intrinsic combinatorial systems, is that of fish belonging to the *Pomacentridae,* and some of their relatives. Inhabitants of coral reefs, these fish are brightly colored. Their markings express partly geometrical combinations, with parallel, perpendicular, or variously angled stripes, alternating colors, circular patches, and so on. These features serve to trigger combative behavior (territorial defense), not sexual relations. As Lorenz has shown, however, this only occurs among the young of a single species; older individuals of the same species become grayish, while colored members of other species are treated as foreign. These data are important for our purposes for two reasons. First, these triggers, like all others, imply a relationship between signifier and signified. Here this relationship does not as yet involve implication, as it will in the case of intrinsic combinatorial systems (see #8), but it does give rise to interesting categorizations consisting in simple dichotomies. For any species A_1 or A_2, etc., the realm of recognizable fishes is divided into two classes: A_1 and A'_1 as opposed to A_2 and A'_2; in other words, "all A's with the same colors and taking the same food" versus "all A"s, i.e., all others including A's that have lost their coloring." Second, these discriminatory reactions are reciprocal. An A_1 which will attack another A_1 violating its territory will also be attacked if it ventures into the other's territory, while both will ignore all A'_1's. We are not here concerned with those relationships between differentiated partners which we are about to discuss, but it should be noted that classification is a first step in the direction of implication.

8. Intrinsic combinatorial systems (process four) have two characteristic features. The first is the presence of combinations embodying such relations as implication of meaning, relations which depend on the "unified-whole" type of structure. The second is the transindividual nature of these hereditary links, most of which involve male, female, and young, or relate to the behavior of social animals. This implies an especially complex organization of the genome, which has to ensure the effective functioning of forms of behavior which are at once differentiated as between individual partners and integrated into a coherent totality founded on their mutual "comprehension."

This category, therefore, does not include all those kinds of behavior that merely imply a signifier-to-signified relationship between a trigger and the action it precipitates—e.g., between a stickleback's perception of the color red in one of its congeners and its initiation of combat. On the other hand, it does cover the more complex cases where actions governed by triggers are also coordinated among themselves by links between their own meanings (i.e., between "signifieds")—cases, in other words, that involve what I am calling meaningful implication. In the familiar instance of *Rissa tridactyla,* already mentioned above (Chapter Three, #4), the striking fact is that a behavioral complex of which both young and adult partake seems to be implied by the placing of the nest on steep cliffs which make the young invulnerable to attack but expose them to the risk of falling. Logically enough, the adults take no precautions against predators while the young do take precautions in moving about the nest. It is fairly obvious, however, that neither is in the habit of performing the logical operation of implicational deduction. The source of the logical link between their respective behaviors must therefore be sought—as in so many other cases—in a physical combinatorial system. The groups of genes responsible for the particular forms of behavior must be linked in a way that corresponds, at the level of unified wholes, with the logical relationship of implication (a relationship which, as I have already pointed out, is also to be found at the much higher, though still physical, level of neuronal connections). Implication here typically means that, where $p \supset q$, the combination "p and not-q" is excluded; in the particular case of *R. tridactyla,* this corresponds exactly to the exclusion of dangerous or useless types of behavior.

In view of a number of observations, we may wonder whether animals do not in some cases become semiconscious of this implicational relationship. Thus, Lorenz has described what he calls *Demut* behavior, an act of submission on the part of the weaker participant designed to disarm a stronger opponent in an unequal fight. The weaker individual, perceiving that he is bound to be defeated, may take up the most dangerous possible posture from his point of view (e.g., a dog will roll over on its back or expose the nape of its neck to its adversary, which does indeed cause the latter to abandon the fight). Such cases exemplify two things: an implicational anticipation of what is about to happen and a coordination between the specific behavior of two individuals. Lorenz has also studied the inverse situation, where without actually starting to fight an animal manifests all the advance warning signals of attack as a way of getting the adversary to back off. In both kinds of cases, assuming—as is seemingly confirmed by its frequency and regularity—that such behavior implies a hereditary factor as well as individual accommodations, the genic combination involved must be accompanied by comprehension at the level of savoir-faire. By contrast, an "instinct" embodying an apparently clear-cut implicational link, but one which the animal itself does not understand, is the "playing dead" so often seen in insects and spiders, the aim being to avoid a danger (when touched, etc.) by mimicking an inanimate object.

As to the transindividual aspects of these implicational links, many cases might be cited. One of the most interesting is the production of pheromones, i.e., hormones which trigger specific and complementary behavior in other individuals belonging to the same animal community or in the sexual partner. The genesis of pheromones and of the coadapted behavior they provoke cannot easily be explained as long as we assume separate evolutions in producing and receiving individuals, and the postulation of a mechanism of transindividual construction is a clear necessity. Another instinctive example is the red patch on the beaks of gulls, which serves the young as a signal announcing the advent of food.[7] In this connection, Wickler wonders which has genetic priority: the formation of the patch in the adult or the demand for it in the young. Wickler defends himself against the charge that this question is meaningless, and Cullen maintains that a specialized adaptation is necessary between this morphogenesis and the pre-existing state of the perceptual apparatus of the young birds. But the basic problem is not that of temporal priority. Rather, we have to understand what kind of transindividual combinatorial system makes possible the correlated construction of a physical signal in the adult and a form of behavior that requires this signal in the young. One thing I am sure of is that this problem will never be solved by appealing to fortuitous mutations modifying the genes themselves,[8] and that the answer has to be sought in intergenic structures whose physical combinations are isomorphic with implication and analogous relationships.

The last point to note here is that the combinatorial systems corresponding to processes three and four may take different forms. We are not exclusively concerned here with Boolean networks, but rather with composite forms in general or with systems of mutual modification capable, among other things, of something resembling what programmers call debugging.

9. The best grounds for skepticism about the mutationist approach is the existence of a fifth formative process common to very many kinds of behavior. This is a compensatory mechanism for dealing with threatening disturbances. All behavioral transformations are in a sense compensatory to the extent that they are adaptive;

any adaptation is a response designed in effect to turn a potential obstacle to advantage, or at the very least to achieve acclimatization to it. But what I want to deal with here are the more specific and instructive cases where an obstacle, though real, is not imposed from without by a new environment but from within by modifications which were dangerous from their inception or which have since become so. I cited a case of this kind at the beginning of this chapter, that of the crawling of slow-worms and ophidians envisaged as a compensation for their apodal characteristics. Here the adaptation plays a reinforcing role in relation to a threatened form of loco-motion. Where such a form has been lost entirely, other compensations are called for. Thus, sea acorns (*Balanus* var.) abandon the capacity for swimming, which is char-acteristic of their larvae *(nauplius),* but compensate for this backward step through the protection afforded by an abode composed of calcareous plaques and through the utilization of their former limbs as organs for capturing and sorting food. Another example is the behavior of the adults and young of some species, where the insufficient development of the young at birth, rendering them more or less nidicolous, has to be compensated for. If they are born with eyes and ears open but with imperfect motor coordination, their need for care is not too great. But when these organs remain closed, and when in addition thermal and motor regulations are inadequate, the im-mature young require intensive nurture. The young of nidifugous species, by contrast, are capable of immediate locomotion once a sufficiently long brooding or gesta-tion period is over.

The case of the pagurians (hermit crabs) would be of

great interest in this connection if it could be shown that a specific form of behavior of theirs, the habit of living in the shells of gastropods, came about after the mutation whereby their abdomens grew dangerously soft. Official doctrine, of course, is that this mutation occurred later, that it could have affected any crabs, and that if the pagurians have survived, it is because they already possessed an instinct for taking up residence in shells. In support of this view the tendency of some crabs to shelter against rocks is evoked; sometimes the animals even carry pebbles about with them for the same purpose. The behavior of pagurians is still very specific and specialized, however, in that these crustaceans do not simply hide in any available crevice; they seek out shells of the exact size they need and change them several times in the course of their growth. Even if this instinct did arise before the softening of the pagurian abdomen, it must surely be acknowledged that it has been consolidated and refined as a result of the need to compensate for the well-nigh lethal dangers to which this mutation exposed the species. And if only this much be granted, we are obliged to ask whether the protective instinct and this mutation might not have arisen from the same formative process.

A spectacular contrasting example worth citing occurs in the balancing organ of some other decapods, where this organ is characterized by a normal cavity equipped with detector hairs, but where the animal has suffered a subtractive mutation leaving it with insufficient statoliths or none at all. Three kinds of compensatory reactions are observable in such cases. The first, a genuine piece of behavior, consists in the animal's taking hold of small pebbles with its anterior pincers (first articulation) and placing them in the cavity or statocyst, where these foreign bodies serve as statoliths. The second, quasibehavioral, solution consists in letting grains of sand get into the statocyst; no active searching goes on here beyond contact with the sand. The third reaction leads to the internal secretion of new statoliths to replace those which have been lost. In all three cases, therefore, compensations occur without our being able to say that the disappearance of the initial statoliths is a result of the reactions in question.

Now, when one process compensates for another, both being hereditary, this certainly implies that the compensatory process is not itself a mutation but rather the result of an overall reaction of an integrated system. In other words, if the effect of a random mutation were compensated for merely by the effects of another mutation at the same level—and hence of the same nature—we should not be dealing with a compensatory mechanism but with another chance event. A compensation in the sense of a corrective readjustment, however, presupposes the existence of a regulatory system indissolubly bound up with an overall dynamics. This has been sufficiently stressed by Weiss from a physiological point of view, and by me in connection with cognitive development, for there to be no need to elaborate further here. Indeed, now that people speak readily of genic homeostasis and of coadaptation of the genome's components, such a view of things may almost be taken as read. My reason for insisting on the point nevertheless is that there is a continuity between the causal compensations that occur in regulatory systems and the logical compensations that ensure equilibrium between affirmations and negations in a complementary network or in any unified whole, etc. This makes it reasonable to treat the compensations that preside over the formation of new specific behavior as yet another expression of a logic immanent to physical reorganizations, and there is thus no need to assign any role here to higher functions.

10. Everything I have suggested up to now is probably fairly acceptable, its entirely speculative character notwithstanding. The situation is different when it comes to the last two processes, which I call complementary reinforcement (process six) and constructive coordination (process seven), both of which seem to play a manifest part in many instincts but neither of which has been satisfactorily accounted for up to now. The types of behavior in question either engender new organs (complementary reinforcements) or display detailed adaptations to external mechanisms which the animal appears to know even though it could not possibly understand them (constructive coordinations), as in the case of the paralyzing stings which *Ammophila* administers to caterpillars destined for its larvae, so immobilizing their nerve centers without killing them. Also falling under this heading is behavior involving the production of toxic substances used for defense (observable at as primitive a level as that of the coelenterate nematocyst). It would of course be presumptuous on my part to venture any explanation of such behavior here. I shall simply try, in the context of my remarks above, to decide what would have to be added to the five processes I have already distinguished if we are to account in terms of physical combinations for mechanisms that are isomorphic with those inventions of the intelligence in which a subject intentionally combines operations in order to resolve a new problem which he has raised himself.

In contrast to the combinatorial systems of processes three and four, which are limited to expressing the consequences of the establishment of links between already constructed elementary forms of behavior, and to the compensations of process five, which consist in the adjustment of unfavorable situations, processes six and seven may be said to be oriented toward goals that are not immediately accessible, or toward the filling of lacks, in accordance with the reinforcements specific to positive feedback systems as opposed to the retroactive effects characteristic of negative ones. An appeal to the mechanism of complementary reinforcement may therefore perhaps supply us with an answer to the question of "invention," but only on condition that this process is seen as operating in the opposite direction from that taken by the processes mentioned previously.

In fact, two levels of complexity have to be distinguished. The simpler one, that of complementary reinforcement, already raises many difficult problems. What happens at this level is that varieties of behavior are improved during phylogenesis through the transformation of organs and through actions embodying genuine inventions, but such behavior remains internal to the organism and to the structuring of actions. An analogy might be drawn, therefore, between the mechanisms of complementary reinforcement and those which, at the level of human behavior, constitute complementary generalizations leading from the sensorimotor schemata of actions to logical operations. The creative nature of such generalizations is based at all levels on the ability to construct new actions or operations on the basis of earlier ones. Complementary reinforcements in animals have as their general aim an increase in the animal's general capacities, but they involve no special access to information about the environment. The best instance is perhaps the evolution of legs (as described by W. Welles) from the hairs or parapods of *Polychaeta* to the six limbs of *Insecta* (via *Peripatus* and *Scutigera*).

By contrast, the level of constructive coordinations (process seven) is much more complex in respect to inventive mechanisms, and it does presuppose information about the environment. It may therefore be compared, in terms of human behavior, to the realm of technical and physical knowledge. The kinds of goals pursued here vary in accordance with highly specialized kinds of actions, and two questions arise. First, how does the animal discover the means required to attain these goals? Second, and just as important, how does it happen to embrace these goals, to discern lacunae which need filling, and thus set out to invent new programs instead of being satisfied with the habits which have hitherto ensured its survival and that of its offspring? Here we touch upon behavior's most characteristic aspect, and its greatest mystery: its need for transcendence, seemingly so at odds with any economic imperatives, and the result of this need, a diversification and complexity of somatic organization that for a long time seemed to run counter to the laws of entropy.

With regard to transcendence in the direction of new goals, the only question which concerns us here, two facts have to be borne in mind from the outset, or the hypotheses I am about to advance are likely to be rejected immediately. The first is that genetic programs, instead of remaining static in respect to their components, and varying only in the combination of these, have become approximately one thousand times richer in elements in the course of evolution. This means that new genes have been brought into being, a quite distinct process from the modifying action of mutations upon pre-existing genes. The second fact is that a single animal may be endowed with two or more behavioral programs or subprograms, although their simultaneous actualization is impossible. The most telling example of this is the tunicates, whose adult behavior is sedentary, the entire body being encased in the "tunic," which remains fast to the ground; nutrition is achieved through filtering, while the larvae, which resemble fish, doubtless display the ancestral form of the vertebrates (tunicates being urochordates). What we have here, then, are two programs or subprograms destined to be realized sequentially, the most important one from the standpoint of the evolutionary line of descent being no more than transitory, epigenetically speaking, but giving rise to a fine example of pedogenesis (of which there are very many).

11. Let us now return to our hypothetical model. Up to this point we have posited two main stages. The first is the formation of elementary types of behavior whose adaptation to the environment may be explained by phenocopies; such behavior is susceptible to certain generalizations (processes one and two). The second is

the constitution of specific complex kinds of behavior by combinatorial systems which orchestrate compatible elementary behavioral forms into a single genetic system; different combinations are produced in this way for each species, however, so that each is assigned to a distinct genome and each has its own program (processes three and four). If this account is correct, it follows logically enough that the next stage (processes six and seven) may result from the bringing together of several *programs*. We would thus have a composite of a higher order or "power"—provided, of course, that the programs so combined belonged to the same genetic system. This situation would differ in two essential ways from the combinatorial systems characterizing the second stage. First, there would be no guarantee at all that programs brought together would be compatible or susceptible to synthesis into a single behavioral form (cf. the two stages mentioned in the case of the tunicates); we thus have a source of conflict, of lacunae, and therefore of the working out of transcendent solutions leading eventually to the emergence of new goals, the framing of which could hardly be explained without the dynamogenic action of disequilibriums of this kind. Second, these disequilibriums and the relationships between the genetic and epigenetic systems would differ from those obtaining in the simpler processes. In the case of phenocopy, the source of elementary behavior, behavior is at first phenotypical and then, where its repetition brings about disequilibriums which end up by making themselves felt in the regulatory genes, the resulting variations are selected by the internal environment as modified by the phenotype at the higher epigenetic levels—hence the convergence between this genic reconstruction and the initial phenotypical behavior. In the third case, on the other hand, where it is two already constituted programs that are brought into conjunction, although their simultaneous realization is impossible, the resulting disequilibrium engenders a transcendent solution as opposed to a copy. The specific task of this new, higher-level combinatorial system is no longer that of orchestrating elementary forms of behavior (adapted to the environment because they derive from phenocopies) in various ways. Rather, its job is to coordinate from two to n epigeneses, each of which derives from a corresponding stage-two combination. Now, since epigenesis interacts at its higher levels with the environment, this composite of epigeneses linked with the programs that are to be transcended will be able to make use of this new information without recourse to phenocopies, though it will employ an analogous mechanism of selective actions exerted by the epigenetic framework upon genic formations. In this respect, the great utility of Temin's "inverse transcriptase" is not that it brings us back to the inheritance of acquired characteristics in the unmediated Lamarckian sense, which I could not endorse; the advantage of this concept is rather that it opens up the possibility of the constitution of new genes according to the sequence DNA→RNA→DNA, which gives rise to "protoviruses." As A. Thomas has noted, "the new sequences formed in this way would undergo selection, chiefly by the specific polymerases and the systems of integration. . . . Thus the protoviruses, equivalent here to 'potentialities,' would play a role in normal cellular differentiation as well as being responsible, in the conversion which eventually produces cancer, for instigating a lasting transformation of the phenotype under the influence of genetic and epigenetic factors." What is involved, therefore, is transformation followed by genetic amplification. "A general mechanism of the variance of the somatic genome would thus have been elucidated."[9] In his "attempt at generalization," Thomas proposes to call such new genes protogenes if they favor normal cellular differentiation rather than carcinogenic aberrations. We might recall in this connection that some biologists, among them Crick and Eigen, feel that DNA's relationship with proteins has been modified in the course of evolution. They hypothesize that the proteins originally provided a matrix for the formation of a DNA, and the predominant DNA→protein relationship expresses the present end result of earlier transformations. These new approaches thus tend to back up Weiss's suppositions concerning formative interaction between the genome and epigenesis, as well as to make my own speculations about the possibilities of a third step founded on such interaction somewhat more plausible. Furthermore, inasmuch as stage-two combinatorial systems are already equipped with structures sophisticated enough to embody the organic equivalent of implication, the transcendent syntheses of this third step may certainly be assumed to encompass those kinds of organization of logical form which are so strikingly reminiscent of the operations of the intelligence, except for the fact that they are limited, physical, and require very little in the way of individual activity on the part of a subject.

12. In concluding these theoretical speculations on instincts, I must emphasize that the seven formative processes I have hypothesized should be treated as themselves dependent on the general dynamics of organization, in that they occur within an organ, the nervous system, which is what integrates them. To the extent, however, that they are also isomorphic with cognitive mechanisms and hypothetically engender instincts which constitute a savoir-faire, a question arises with which we have not yet dealt. It concerns the nature of the link which binds genes together in a physical combinatorial system while at the same time conveying the sense of implication or of some other epistemic relationship. In my opinion, the solution to this problem will have to be sought in the vicinity of the very unusual connections that typify the earliest epigenetic syntheses. Jacques Monod describes these connections as "stereospecific discrimination," and suggests that a set of interlocking meanings, complete with implications, is a reflection in such cases of the interlocking spatial forms which make up this physical combinatorial system. Be that as it may, I have no more intention of proffering explanations here than elsewhere in this chapter. Given the primitive state of our knowledge in this sphere, the rush to explanation inevitably smacks of an alarming ingenuousness. Nevertheless, I hope to have shown that it makes a good deal of sense to try and conceive of the cognitive structure of that behavior which most closely parallels sophisticated intelligent operations in organic and physical terms. In short, I have tried to justify the idea of a "logic of the organs" from which instincts may be said to derive prior to the emergence of the "logic of actions" characterizing the levels of sensorimotor acquisition, and *a fortiori* long in advance of the "logic of concepts" specific to the higher forms of intelligence.[10]

Notes to Chapter Seven

1. The fact that human "reason" thus falls into the category of the instinctive is not as problematic as it might at first appear, for while it is true that its structures are constructed, there is no doubt that its functioning presupposes the existence of innate nervous mechanisms.

2. According to A. Raynaud, the "somites" which normally serve as the embryogenetic inductors of reptilian members lose this capacity in apoda, even though they are more numerous here than in tetrapods.

3. Martin John Wells, *Lower Animals* (New York: McGraw-Hill, 1968), p. 198.

4. A. Etienne, "Le problème de la motivation en éthologie." *Arch. Psych.* (1974), 52, p. 368.

5. W. Wickler, "Vergleigende Verhaltensforschung und Phylogenetik." In G. Heborer, *Die Evolution der Organismen* (1967), vol. 1.

6. Witt, Reed, and Peakall, *A Spider's Web* (New York: Springer-Verlag, 1968).

7. The red patch in question is located at the extremity of the beak (as, for example, in *Larus argentatus*). The young strike this spot, and this triggers the regurgitation of food by the adult. See the work of Goethe (1937), Tinbergen and Perdeck (1950), and Hailman (1967).

8. Unless one is going to posit the formation of organizing genes responsible for the combination of subgroups of others.

9. *Comptes rendus des séances de l'Académie des Sciences*, Dec. 8, 1971.

10. This book was already in press when I received J.-P.

Changeux's opening lecture at the Collège de France. Had this contribution reached me earlier, I should certainly have cited it in detail because of Changeux's conception of a "functional epigenesis giving rise to an economy of the genes," in that "activity introduces an additional dimension into the developing network. (The genetic envelope constitutes a network with indeterminate outlines; activity is what fills in the angles.)" And I should most certainly have referred to his account according to which the organism, through learning, "becomes receptive to a combinatorial system of signs which it is also able to produce itself."

EIGHT

Some Remarks on Plant Behavior

IF WE CONTINUE to define behavior, as we have up to now, as goal-directed action designed to use or transform the environment, or to modify the organism's situation vis-à-vis the environment, then it is clear that there is such a thing as plant behavior, and indeed that all the processes formative of instincts that we have described, even the seventh, occur in the plant kingdom. One does not have to speak, like Maeterlinck, in terms of an "intelligence of flowers" to acknowledge that in the case of the *Orchidaceae,* where self-pollination is not generally possible but where the flowers are so organized that insects transport the two masses of pollen known as pollinia from one flower to the next, we have clear evidence of constructive mechanisms in which the formation of organs is intimately bound up with what, since insects are part of the orchid's external environment, can only be called behavior. By contrast, as I have already noted in the Introduction, I would not class as behavior the production of oxygen or causal modifications of the biotope involving no formative teleonomy.

•   •   •

1. The existence of behavior in plants is thus incontestable, particularly when movements are involved, but such behavior is nevertheless formally limited in three ways which are of great importance when it comes to the general problem of causal relationships between behavior and evolutionary changes (i.e., when morphogenesis as well as selection is under consideration). The first of these limitations is the absence of locomotion. Exceptions here are the dispersal of seeds and the rotation on sloping terrain of the small globular shoots that *Sempervivum soboliferum* produces with its asexual reproduction. But a passive rather than an active mobility is operative in such cases; the movements of plants are merely local or partial movements of particular parts of an organism which is in any event attached to the ground, not overall displacements of a body changing its position in space. This first limitation is accompanied by a second, just as basic. This is the absence of a nervous system, and it is hard to say whether this is the cause or the outcome of the lack of locomotion. That the two limitations are closely related becomes very clear if one envisages the nervous system as a sort of concretization of the links called for by behavior. The third limitation of plant behavior also has a close kinship with the first two. Behavior in general we have defined as action exerted upon the environment or action designed to modify the organism's functional situation in relation to the environment, but obviously plants do not act upon the environment by transporting objects, etc. Rather, they act only upon themselves, seeking thereby to strengthen or establish vital links with the environment. Turning toward the light, adapting flowers to the behavior of insects, ensuring the dispersal of seeds by a host of mechanisms —these all exemplify behavior limited in this way. It is genuine behavior in that it is directed at the environment. At the same time, it is limited in that the movements of external objects are not determined, each separately, by a direct causality originating in the organism (with a few rare exceptions; e.g., the carnivorous *Drosera*). Instead, these movements are, so to speak, solicited and then utilized by the plant's design, which is generated and genetically programmed according to an overall plan.

A comparison of plant behavior with the mobility of animals, with the progressive role of a nervous system displaying the most varied degrees of refinement, and with action upon the environment effected by means of a buccal orifice with its manifold structures and accessory features (dentition, beak, etc.), or by means of specialized limbs, reveals the striking difference—due to these three limitations—between the evolution of the plant kingdom and that of the animal kingdom. This difference is epitomized by the relative absence—aside from the important division between phanerogams and cryptogams—of any major transformations in plant evolution. No doubt the formation of chloroplasts in the transition from schizophytes to thallophytes, that of stalks and leaves in bryophytes, or that of a vascular apparatus in pteridophytes, represents so many evolutionary steps comparable to those made by the first subkingdoms of invertebrates. It is also true that the improved protection of ovules embodied in the advance from gymnospermy to angiospermy expresses a tendency toward autonomy from the environment, as does the improvement of the reproductive organs of seeds between early phenerogams such as the cycads and their more highly evolved descendants. Yet this independence from the surroundings is a far cry from that achieved by the vertebrates or even by the lower invertebrates. Furthermore, neither gymnosperms like the conifers, nor angiosperms like the oaks, birches, or poplars (to take three distinct families), ever display a hierarchy of levels such as that which separates worms from arthropods, for instance. Nor is it possible, among angiosperms, to discern any major gradation in levels of refinement between, say, dicotyledons like the *Rosaceae* and monocotyledons like the *Liliaceae.* Such differentiated levels are even harder to find between apetalous, dialypetalous, and gamopetalous dicotyledons. In short, one is hard put to locate gulfs in the plant world comparable to those that mark off coelenterates or echinoderms from birds or mammals, and there is simply no equivalent in the plant kingdom for the primates. As for the very real differences between cryptogams and phanerogams, these are due to the formation of precisely those organs whose functioning is the most closely bound up with what may and must be called plant behavior: flowering, fertilization, and seed propagation are based on an interaction with the environment, the dynamics of which is largely extrasomatic and clearly distinct from the physicochemical metabolism.

Thus, my principal thesis here concerning the formative role of behavior in evolutionary processes is lent support by evidence from the world of plants in the shape of what might be called a negative verification: the relative paucity of hierarchy and evolutionary progress because of the limitations of behavior, coupled with the presence of these characteristics in the one area where behavior is, atypically, well developed.

2. It is all the more interesting, therefore, to find that despite the above mentioned limitations, the plant kingdom offers evidence of all of the seven formative processes which seemed in animals to characterize the establishment of instincts and which here apparently inform the functioning of organs or morphogenetic phenomena comparable to specific behavior.

Let us begin with the transition from successions to anticipations. I myself have examined a particular aspect of what could be called a kind of behavior among species of *Sedum* and among *Crassulaceae* in general.[1] What we find here is a vegetative reproduction by means of a dehiscence of sterile branches, which fall to the ground and immediately put down adventitious roots. This shedding of branches is prepared for by an anticipatory mechanism observable, at least in some species, from the beginning of the branch's growth; shrinkage occurs, splits appear, and things are so arranged that after a certain point the slightest disturbance (e.g., rain or passing grasshoppers) will cause the branch to fall off. Seeking to explain this phenomenon without appealing to final causes (as distinct from a teleology bound up with a causal mechanism), I tried to determine whether such anticipations were derived from earlier successions of events. I found that the process does indeed begin below ground level, where rhizomes or roots vigorous enough to become independent of the mother plant exhibit the same separation process, although this is not yet anticipatory in character because it is based on an already acquired autonomy. The mechanism is then transferred to ground shoots and eventually to aerial branches.

Such data therefore reveal a transition from succession to anticipation. They further indicate an element of generalization in that transfers occur. Other instances of generalization could easily be cited—for example, the production of axillary bulblets, as in *Lilium bulbiferum*, which develops these on its upper leaves although the starting point of the asexual reproduction of lilies is of course the underground division of bulbs.

Combination processes are also to be found in the plant kingdom. An example is the multiple variations in the flower of the *Orchidaceae*. This flower is one of the most complex in existence, and the differences between one species and its closest relative, as in the *Ophrys* family, bring to mind our earlier discussion of the variety of extrinsic combinatorial systems (process three). As for intrinsic combinatorial systems with implicational connections (process four), the most striking datum here is doubtless the formation of seeds. The variability of seeds depends in any case on an *extrinsic* combinatorial system, but there is also an implicational link between the traits that act in concert to ensure dissemination. In the case of wind-dispersed seeds, the problem is how to reconcile lightness with a morphology suited to the exploitation of the air's action; hence the wing-like appendages, etc., the many forms of which are so familiar. Where dispersal depends on animals, as in the case of the kernels of fleshy fruits (cherries, etc.), the important thing is that the kernel be sturdy enough to survive the effects of the animal's digestive processes and of transportation in its excrement. In short, each kind of seed embodies not only particular refinements in the differentiation of characteristics, but also an equally great refinement in these characteristics' interconnections, which constitute the materialization of a sort of implicational system.

As for compensations, two kinds are worth mentioning here. The first merely involves reactions to disturbances in the environment; the second also mobilizes behavior designed to make up for a lack for which the species' hereditary characteristics are responsible. An example of the first kind of compensation is supplied by several varieties of *Sedum sediforme* that differ from the species-specific blue-green type, which thrives in full sunlight in the Mediterranean region, in that they exhibit an increase in chlorophyll and in photosynthetic capacity when in the shade or in unfavorable conditions. Obviously, it is not the lack of light which makes these plants greener, but rather a compensatory reaction to this situation. The second kind of compensation is exemplified by the curious behavior of *Sedum amplexicaule,* which in contrast to all other members of the *Sedum* genus has a low tolerance for the heat (and possibly the dryness) of summertime. In the hot season it dries up completely, loses its leaves, and takes on the shriveled, faded, and desiccated appearance of a dead plant. As soon as autumn arrives, however, new leaves appear and the plant becomes green once more; and in the spring, it produces fine yellow flowers, the whole plant now being far larger than the summer's relic. What we have here, then, as with the animals mentioned earlier, is a hereditary variation with two aspects, one posing a threat to survival and the other compensating for it.

Lastly, unexplained innovations achieving adaption through adequation to differentiated environmental conditions are of course legion in the plant kingdom, the most spectacular instance perhaps being the different modes of fertilization.

This is not the place to discuss the various reactions of plants to light[2] (tropisms, taxis, nastic responses), etc., because we are not concerned here with the nature of particular forms of behavior but only with behavior's relationship to evolution. I would merely draw attention to the fact that we naturally find the same phenocopy process in plants as in animals. (We have already looked at this process in *Sedum album* and *S. sediforme,* where a hereditary decrease in size follows the formation of phenotypes expressing this characteristic.) We also encounter the same problems concerning complex combinations of elementary reactions. All I have been able to do in these few remarks on plants is to stress the important differences between the plant and animal kingdoms in respect to our general problem, and at the same time to point up the existence in the plant world, despite these overall differences, of the same basic formative processes found in animals.

Notes to Chapter Eight

1. Jean Piaget, "Observations sur le mode d'insertion et la chute des rameaux secondaires chez les *Sedum.*" *Candollea* (1966), 21–22, pp. 137–239.
2. A question studied as early as the work of Augustin-Pyrame de Candolle.

NINE

General Conclusions:
Behavior, Motor of Evolution

I HAVE ALREADY cited a passage in which Jacques
Monod, displaying uncompromising logic and rare
"philosophical courage" in defense of his ideas on
chance, maintains that since the essential characteristic
of living things is their "conservative mechanism,"
evolution can only be explained in terms of "imperfections" in this mechanism. If one accepts the hypothesis that chance mutations are the sole source of
evolutionary changes, Monod's position is indeed
unassailable. As soon as such a completely chance-
based genetics is deemed inadequate, however, the
tendency toward conservation implies the necessity of
transformations. The organism is an open system, a
necessary precondition of whose functioning is behavior; and (if there is so much as a germ of truth in the
tentative hypotheses I have advanced above) it is of
the essence of behavior that it is forever attempting to
transcend itself and that it thus supplies evolution
with its principal motor.

•   •   •

1. My closing remarks here, therefore, will not be confined to recalling the clear role of behavior in survival and in all kinds of selection, for I shall further conclude that it is behavior itself, by virtue of the very demands it makes, that is always responsible, throughout phylogenesis, for the far-reaching morphogenetic changes of macro-evolution. True enough, the biophysical and biochemical processes involved in the maintenance of the living organism's internal organization would have no reason of their own to change (as Monod rightly asserts) were it not for the impact of aborted efforts at conservation as manifested by mutations. Observation indeed confirms that these processes have remained remarkably stable, from micro-organisms to man. Yet despite this stability of the fundamental physicochemical life processes, an unexplained phenomenon remains—namely, the substantial increase in the number of genes, from the bacteria to the higher vertebrates.[1] It thus seems impossible to avoid the conclusion that the reasons for evolution must be sought at a level other than that of the mechanisms of reproduction alone. If the organism is an "open" system, the problem has to be located within the relationship between this system's relative openness and its functional closure in the form of cycles; the two factors are equally important to the system's self-conservation, but their interactions are subject to constant evolutionary variation precisely because openings as well as the tendency toward closure exist.

This is where behavior enters the picture, both as the expression of the overall dynamics of organization in its interaction with the environment and as a source of supersessions and innovations for as long as the environment or environments continue to contain any elements creating obstacles for the organism. In describing the process which makes behavior constantly innovative in this way in the transition from any given species or taxonomic group to another, we need to call once more upon the general notions of assimilation and accommodation evoked in Chapter One. These notions apply as readily to the organism's interactions with the outside as to behavioral forms themselves. In relation to such interactions, assimilation in the broad sense is an incorporation of substances or energies tending to conserve the system; and where the resulting metabolism effectively performs this task, there will be no need for changes unless accommodation to a new environment is obligatory. In relation to behavior, we may use the same term "assimilation" to refer to the integration of objects into the schemata of actions (the integration of all the intermediaries between actions and physiological assimilation; e.g., between the search for food and its digestion). There are thus as many types of assimilation as there are types of behavior (including the perception of dangers as well as the perception of useful objects, etc.). Consequently, the outer limits of praxic assimilation can only expand, in function of the advance from behavior based on contact to that based on long-range action, or from effectuations to anticipations and precautionary measures. Furthermore—and this is a point of fundamental import—where physiological assimilation proceeds by simple repetition, without reference to earlier phases, behavioral assimilation engenders a memory which increases the number of relationships and thus contributes to its own extension. As for accommodations imposed by external variations which modify assimilation in varying degrees, these are merely suffered passively by the physiological organization and result only in replacements, always kept to a minimum, of particular aspects of an assimilatory cycle. By contrast, the accommodation of action schemata is a source of refinements that do not abolish the established behavioral forms but differentiate them through the introduction of subsystems.

In short, when we compare the basic functional mechanisms common to physiology and behavior, we find a systematic contrast between the conservative tendencies which predominate in the physiological realm and the expansionist factors which in the realm of behavior push assimilation and accommodation combined toward what appears to constitute behavior's dual goal on all levels: to widen the environment and to increase the living organism's capacities. What this amounts to is that physiologically a lower-order species, a sponge or a starfish, is just as perfectly adapted to its environment as a higher-order species, a crow or a fox. Behaviorally, however, further progress can always be made. Sponges would benefit from better techniques for perception at a distance, for their movements of contraction and expansion, or for the orientation of the trajectories of their amoebocytes (mobile message-bearing cells); while in vertebrates, curiosity and the fueling of action schemata in themselves constitute factors favoring the permanent possibility of improvements.

2. We are thus able to claim that while the organism has no reason to generate variations, it is of the essence of behavior that it strives to improve and hence to transcend itself; but we cannot directly infer from this that the motor of evolutionary transformations must lie in behavior. We have first to deal with the preliminary question of the nervous system's dual role, for this system is at once the precondition of behavioral progress and the reflection of a total physiological organization to whose integration it contributes in return. It is thus quite reasonable to entertain the notion that, phylogenetically speaking, it is the development of the nervous system, itself attributable to the development of an overall organization, that precipitates advances in behavior, even including behavior's inherent tendencies toward self-transcendence. As a matter of fact, most authors have tended to embrace this view of things. Serious arguments may nevertheless be adduced for reversing this account and envisaging the nervous system as the concretization of all the behavioral forms possible at a given stage. In the first place, it is well known that before the nervous system's emergence in the coelenterates, there already exist cells sensitive to external stimuli, and others specifically involved in the animal's movements. Any strengthening of these activities in these circumstances might be expected to induce both an increased differentiation with regard to cellular function and the establishment of intercellular links, and here we would have the first fibers of a nascent nervous system, with a minimum of connections and as yet no centralization. With the beginnings of predation, especially, we would see the coordination of movements —in the initially very limited form of haphazard motions achieving linear directedness only in the vicinity of stimuli—along with sensory coordinations leading to the formation of ganglia, and so on.

Secondly, the development of nerve centers seems to follow rather than dictate the development of some forms of behavior even in the higher animals. Paillard has shown that in herbivorous mammals the mouth's prehensile action is better represented in the cortex than the motor action of the anterior limbs, whereas the opposite is true in cats and monkeys.

Thirdly, research on nervous plasticity, the results of which have for so long been alternately negative and positive on the question of whether or not nerve endings join up in the event of accidental or induced lacunae in the synapses, recently produced the instructive conclusion (cf., the work of Teuber and his group at MIT) that systematic restoration occurs so long as functioning has not been stabilized; once this stage is reached, however, such plasticity is no longer observed. Other well-known results relevant here are those of Rosenzweig and Kretch concerning the thickening of axons in rats in the event of stimulating activity, and the findings of the great deal of research done on the reorganization of nerve circuitry in crabs and insects after the loss of one or more limbs.

What this variety of data tends to show is that, even if the development of the nervous system is not the direct outcome of the development of behavior, there is at any rate a very close interaction between these two evolutions—an interaction such that the initiatives come from behavior despite the fact that the nervous system supplies behavior with its tools. The remarkable thing here is that whereas nutrition, respiration, circulation, and reproduction are represented at all stages, the nervous function emerges belatedly but then proceeds to make such strides—from the fibers of coelenterates to the hominian brain—as to easily outstrip, relatively speaking, the advances made by the other functions. It is very hard indeed to account for this superiority of the nervous system without invoking behavior's continuous creativity. Moreover, nervous activity has two orientations. In the first place, it is directed outward, extending its capacities, in tandem with those of behavior, in an ever-broadening environment; secondly, it is directed inward in order to coordinate the organs. Both these forms of activity are predicated on the same unitary advances, so that each is essential to the other. So it is legitimate to infer that inasmuch as behavior plays a role in the formation of the nervous system, it helps generate the overall organization of which it is at the same time an expression.

3. This brings us to the heart of our problem, to the relationship between the evolution of forms and organs and that of behavior. Here two propositions seem inescapable. The first is a platitude questioned by no one: the correlation between morphology and behavior at every phylogenetic stage. The second is upheld by a few independent-minded people but runs counter to the general view. This is the idea that it is impossible to explain the great transformations characterizing macro-evolution solely by reference to the interplay between mutations and "recombinations."

Now, there clearly has to be a link between these two propositions. With regard to the first, just a few points will suffice. Broadly speaking, animals that do not go in search of food but wait for it to come to them haphazardly are of radiate symmetry, like the great majority of sedentary species and also the *Medusae* which, though pelagic, confine themselves to catching the plankton that enters their mouths. By contrast, animals that actively seek out their subsistence are elongated and their symmetry is a bilateral one. Even among the coelenterates, the siphonophores, which are akin to the *Medusae,* live in colonies of long ovoid form, snapping up their prey with their tentacles as they float around. As a general rule, behavioral advances are marked by an increase in the number of movements possible for the animal and in its mobility within the environment, and these developments lead to a set of neurological and morphological refinements. It is difficult to think of a more striking multiple exemplification of this process than the molluscs: thus lamellibranchiates, which are immobile or move very little, exhibit very primitive behavior (we have already discussed their filter-based nutritional system); gastropods, which enjoy greater independence because of their mobility, are more differentiated behaviorally and nutritionally, often mastering novel environments, for example, although they are still fairly simple animals; and cephalopods, which are highly mobile, and gifted swimmers, predators and so on, are endowed, thanks to a sudden and spectacular advance, with a refined central nervous system and sophisticated sense organs, including eyes comparable to those of vertebrates. In other subkingdoms, the deployment of behavior in parallel with growing mobility determines a series of transformations of the internal as well as the external aspects of organization: limbless movements are superseded by the manifold forms of locomotion calling for the development of fins, legs, and wings, and their corollary nervous apparatuses and musculatures—all changes affecting anatomy in its most essential aspects. In this connection I would merely point out that the use of limbs requires solid points of purchase and a certain rigidity of body, whence comes the multiplicity of solutions found by the arthropods and vertebrates.

All of this is undisputed common knowledge. What is surprising, in the present state of biology, is the fact that, while everyone acknowledges our complete experimental ignorance regarding the mechanism of variations other than intraspecific ones, it is not generally seen as obvious that this problem is dominated by a preliminary alternative that may be expressed as follows: *Either* organs come into being independently of behavior, both being the result of mutations, so that we have two more or less autonomous sets of chance occurrences which it falls to selection alone to reconcile and at the same time to adapt to the external environment; *or else* organs and behavior are of necessity coordinated from the very moment of their inception, in which case behavior must play the principal role in this process, in the first place because it is the precondition of the necessary interaction between environment and organism (the metabolism in the broad sense of the term), and secondly because only behavior is in a position to govern the improvement or supersession of adaptations. In sum, either chance and selection can explain everything or else behavior is the motor of evolution. The choice is between an alarming waste in the shape of multitudinous and fruitless trials preceding any success no matter how modest, and a dynamics with an internal logic deriving from those general characteristics of organization and self-regulation peculiar to all living things.

4. I should like to conclude these brief and no doubt incautious remarks by offering a summary of my argument focussed on the core of the problem: the intrinsically adaptive nature of behavior. Far be it from me to deny that some evolutionary variations may be the outcome of chance and selection as normally understood. *Littorina* and many other gastropods of the Atlantic coast, for example, have shells sturdy enough to guarantee them complete safety in the rough waters they encounter with each tide, and it is perfectly plausible that the thickness of their test was produced by a random mutation, and that a continuous selection process eliminated individuals with thin shells, so canalizing the more resistant toward the state in which we now find these species. The question, however, is whether this paradigm can meaningfully be applied to the genesis of behavior. For example, inasmuch as the three prerequisites of an adapted bird's nest are its solidity, the protection it affords against predators, and its capacity to maintain a certain temperature, are we going to assume that in the case of the common swallow, say, there were once pairs which, under the influence of one of a range of mutations, built frail nests in perilous locations and left them full of holes for drafts to blow through, and that such behavior continued until the occurrence of happier mutations made possible the selection of more skillful individuals and the elimination of the inept? Obviously not. The emergence of any specific behavior may of course involve trial and error, but this procedure is itself subject to the three requirements characteristic of behavior's unique situation among evolutionary mechanisms. For behavior must manifest an intrinsic adaptation from three points of view: from the point of view of its teleonomy; from the point of view of its specialized adequations; and from the point of view of the particular role played by selections effected by the internal environment as mediator between the external environment and the orientation of new variations. It seems to me that the conjunction of these three characteristics is what makes behavior a motor force in evolution.

The first aspect, then, is teleonomic. Since behavior, I repeat, is action exerted upon the environment aiming from the moment of its initiation to produce results in the outside world, it cannot be compared to a random mutation generated quite independently of the environment and destined to be accepted or rejected by this environment after the fact and in the light of unprogrammed outcomes. Because this goal-directedness of behavior is essential to the organism's vital needs, and thus intrinsic to its overall dynamics, it requires from the outset detailed information about the environment toward which actions are to be oriented.

The second aspect of the intrinsic nature of adaptations of behavior is a corollary of the first. It is the development of a savoir-faire isomorphic with a cognitive system. In this respect such adaptations are quite distinct from adaptations or selections which retain the "fittest" from the point of view of survival alone. "Survival"-type selection deals with individuals on the basis of their sturdiness and reproductive capacity, whereas adaptation through adequation selects experiments or actions as such, according to the criterion of their success as judged in relation to the specific goals pursued. True, behavioral adaptations always tend to foster preservation and survival in the end, but they are also rich in specific accommodations, and above all in the ever-present potential for transcendence.

The adaptation peculiar to behavior is thus intrinsic by virtue both of its teleonomy and of its "precognitive" structures. It is also intrinsic in a third sense related to the selective role of the internal environment. In order to account for the manifest correlation between specific behavior or instincts, on the one hand, and the particular aspects of the environments upon which they act, on the other, while at the same time avoiding the Lamarckian notion of direct action, I have advanced two complementary hypotheses. The first is that elementary forms of behavior are acquired on the phenotypical level and that the internal environment, once modified by these acquisitions, proceeds to select genic variations until a phenocopy reconstructing actions in function of this new framework is endogenously produced. The second hypothesis is that complex instincts derive from a genic combinatorial system that synthesizes elementary forms of behavior and eventually transcends them by means of complementary reinforcements, a process which also presupposes a selective action on the part of the epigenetic environment.

Differing in these three essential ways, then, from ordinary variations, the formation of behavior certainly appears to constitute a mechanism made unique by its mediated yet continuous relationship with the environment.

This is why, in contrast to the conservative tendencies characterizing the internal organization of living things, behavior must be deemed the principal factor in evolution. To the extent that evolutionary "progress" depends at once on the growth of the power of organisms over their environment and on the relative independence they acquire as a result of their actions—an independence which, as already noted, is largely due to an increased mobility—behavior must be considered the motor of all these transformations. And, no matter how neurological, physiological, or even biochemical the preconditions of behavior may be, the fact remains that behavior itself creates those higher unitary activities without which macro-evolution would be incomprehensible.

5. We have yet to try and understand the relationship between the two kinds of evolution we have been led to distinguish. The first kind might be described as an "organizing" evolution, and it applies to behavior as well as to the differentiated organs behavior requires. The second is that "variational" evolution which through the interplay of mutations and sexual recombinations introduces variations into already organized systems.

This relationship is far from simple. For one thing, the known laws of genetics, which govern variational evolution, adequately account for phenomena which occur over very long periods of time and are thus also an aspect of macro-evolution. In both plant and animal evolution, for instance, an overall acceleration has occurred, as attested by the ever-decreasing time lapses, chronologically, between the emergence of one subkingdom and that of a later, more highly evolved one; and this general acceleration is apparently to be explained by genetic recombinations in the case of sexual reproduction. Again, the formation of a new species, never observed at a mutational level, seems to be the outcome of limitations upon the circulation of genetic information within populations, and is a process taking millennia, as opposed to the brief three-quarters of a century during which mutations have been studied. In both these cases, therefore, a genetics of recombined genomes and of populations seems capable of accounting for the mechanisms involved. On the other hand, those transformations in hereditary behavior which seem to be the wellspring of organizing evolution may consist in limited modifications—albeit open to new possibilities—as easily as of changes of great scope. It is not the quantitative aspect of these processes that supplies us with a yardstick, but rather a qualitative factor.

What I call "variational" evolution thus affects modifications in already formed genetic and epigenetic systems whose internal teleonomy is in need of preservation. The variations produced in this way may be random and are only controlled by the environment to the extent that they are subject to an *a posteriori* selection. By contrast, I speak of "organizing" evolution where developments are subordinated from the outset to two teleonomies, one internal and the other relating to the environment. In other words, these developments are both conditioned by the needs of action upon the environment and precipitated by the gaps which need filling in order to ensure the operation of such action.

Organizing evolution governs the constitution of new hereditary behavioral forms and of those organs which serve as the instruments of such behavior. But it is important to note that we speak here of "instruments" and not "conditions": respiration, nutrition, and the like are conditions of behavior, and although they already involve interaction with the environment (albeit physico-chemical interaction), they do not constitute the *instruments* of actions exerted *upon* the environment in the sense that legs, wings, or even eyes may be said to be the instruments of locomotor or exploratory actions. This distinction will perhaps strike some as overwrought, and it is true that in a loose sense one might call the lungs the instruments of respiratory action. But I have always reserved the term "actions" for activity directed toward specific and modifiable objects. Actions so understood are always informed by teleonomies differentiated in function of such variable objects, which remain outside the somatic sphere for the duration of the action in question. Even in the case of nutrition, it is easy enough to distinguish between the actions involved in the search for food or the pursuit of prey, each of which calls for a new accommodation, and the physiological processes which begin with ingestion. Perception itself may be said from this point of view to be subordinate to action to the extent that it invests objects with practical meanings. (As von Weizsacker remarked a long time ago, to perceive a house is not to see an object that is entering your eye but an object that you yourself are about to enter.) In contrast to respiration or to the alimentary metabolism, which are based on a repetition or recurrence, located, naturally, within a pre-existing but permanent internal teleonomy, action presupposes a certain "precursive" capacity, the capacity to bring each phase into relation with the following one in function of an existing goal which is revised with every fresh situation by means of differentiated teleonomies centered on objects external to the organism.

It should now be clear that while the formation of new behavior cannot occur on the basis of a chance-governed genetics, because it is subordinated to both an internal and an external teleonomy, with the latter intervening from the inception of each new formation and not as the outcome of a *posteriori* selection, behavior must for this very reason require an adaptation, through adequation, of its specific organic instruments. Inasmuch as hereditary behavior expresses a sort of organic logic, as I sought to show in Chapter Seven by describing the seven principal formative mechanisms of instinctive behavior, it follows that those organs serving as indispensable instruments of behavior must depend on the same formative process.

My justification for positing a unity of this kind between behavior and its instrumental organs is, of course, to be found in the above arguments concerning teleonomy. The formation of behavior cannot be fortuitous because it is governed from the start by an external teleonomy, so the same must hold true for the organs this behavior needs, though of course they may be perfected only gradually. Jacques Monod, a biologist who can scarcely be suspected of wishing to minimize the role of chance, seems himself to make an exception in the case of behavior and its attendant organs: "The fact that in the evolution of certain groups one observes a general tendency, maintained over millions of years, toward the apparently oriented development of certain organs shows how the initial choice of a certain kind of behavior . . . commits the species irrevocably in the direction of a continuous perfecting of the structures and perform-ances this behavior needs for its support."[2] And after giving the example, already cited above, of that sup-posed ancestor of four-legged vertebrates, a primitive fish that "chose" to explore terra firma, Monod proceeds to evoke the famous case of the orthogenesis of the horse's hoof, said to have been determined by the fact that "the ancestors of the horse at an early point chose to live upon open plains and to flee at the approach of an enemy (rather than put up a fight or hide)."

It will doubtless be objected that the alliance I am postulating between organ and behavior amounts to a reversion to the Lamarckian axiom that the "function creates the organ," a claim which assumes a direct envi-ronmental action upon genetic mechanisms. In answer to this charge, I would point out first of all that even the most orthodox neo-Darwinian in no way reduces the role of the environment or of the necessity of adaptation to any environment; he is content to replace the simple and immediate causal action in which Lamarck believed with a probabilistic and retroactive action based exclusively on selection. All I have tried to do here in this connection is draw a distinction between selection based on adequa-tion and selection based on survival (or differential re-production), and then account for the former in terms of the selective effects of the internal and epigenetic envi-ronment as modified by phenotypical traits generated through interaction with the external environment. Here again it is worth quoting Monod, when he maintains so correctly that the selective theory has "been too often understood or represented as placing the sole responsibility for selection upon conditions of the external environment. This is a completely mistaken conception. For the selective pressures . . . are in no case unconnected with the teleonomic performances characteristic of the species. . . . [It is] specific interactions, which the organism itself 'elects,' at least in part, [that] determine the nature and orientation of the selective pressure the organism sustains."[3] In my terminology, this amounts to saying that although the formulation the "function creates the organ" remains true at the phenotypical level, a fact everywhere confirmed by observation, and although phenotypes modify the internal environment, it is the resulting new framework that selectively governs the hereditary variations produced in the event of disequilibrium. Whether we should speak here of the Baldwin effect, of genetic assimilation, or of phenocopy as described in Chapter Six, is an open question. The main point, however, is that the postulation of such a genetic reconstruction of learned or chosen behavior, and of its motor role in the macro-evolution of behavior's executive organs, is quite consistent with an account based on selection, and in no way implies a direct environmental action in the Lamarckian sense. After all, action by the environment and action upon the environment are very different things. The refinement I propose in our picture of the selective mechanism tends precisely to place this mechanism in the service of the organism's activities and choices, while removing it from the influence of the chance factors that play such a large part in variational evolution. It is over the question of the role of chance, therefore, that I part company with neo-Darwinism, and in taking the view that the organism's activity extends to directed or combinatorial mechanisms essential to the formation of behavior, like the seven general processes described in Chapter Seven. As for the question of interactions between epigenesis and the genome, where I have endeavored to stay within the bounds of a caution dictated by our ignorance, it remains to be seen whether or not the findings of Temin or others can lend support to the general orientation of my thesis.

It is from the study of interactions of this kind, in fact, that we may expect future advances in genetics to arise, as well, perhaps, as some explanation of the relationship between what I have called the variational and organizing types of evolution. Meanwhile, in trying to grasp the nature of this relationship, we shall have to be satisfied with the analogy of the problems encountered in artificial programming. Here, as in genetic programming, the question arises of what conditions have to be met in order to modify the program in one specific detail. Conceivably, the solution arrived at by computer technology may help us explain the necessity, in accounting for the formation of new behavior, of evoking a combinatorial system of a higher order than the one constituted by the interactions of mutations and sexual recombinations. In a computer capable of performing 40,000 simple operations (a still modest total), two distinct kinds of "language" are needed to convey programming instructions: a "machine language" dealing with simple operations and "higher languages" embodying essential systems of subordinations and hierarchies. Using the machine language alone does not suffice for introducing a modification at a specific point in the program, but by calling upon the higher languages it is possible to isolate the location of the variation required by means of successive approximations. If we compare the genes, and their mutations and combinations, to the machine language, it is clear that the maintenance of the connections between epigenesis and the genome, as required for the constitution of new behavior, will call for a structuring capacity analogous to that of the higher computer languages with their hierarchies. These in no way negate the links specific to the machine language; rather, they supplement them in an indispensable way when it is necessary to modify a specific detail of the conditions of a complex program in an "adequate" manner.

If such analogies seem farfetched,[4] perhaps it will make the complementarity of the organizing and variational kinds of evolution more comprehensible if I once more evoke Paul A. Weiss's central conception: the necessity of positing an overall dynamics in accounting for the effects of those "systems" that characterize forms of behavior just as they characterize the general organization of every living thing. Interactions between genes alone cannot explain such systems, because their "supragenic" and "organic matrix," as constituted by the organism as a whole, has existed from the start and has been passed down without interruption from the earliest living beings. The fact is that if we accept a "dualism" of this kind between the respective (and in other respects complementary) actions of an overall dynamics on the one hand and subgroups of "discrete units" on the other

(cf., Chapter Five, #2), we cannot avoid two logical conclusions—although unfortunately we can only reach
them by speculative means for the time being. The first
is that there is an organizing evolution as well as a variational one; and the second is that behavior is its motor.

Notes to Chapter Nine

1. I have already mentioned (Chapter Seven, #2) the hypotheses of Temin and Thomas regarding the formation of new genes through inverse transcriptase.

2. Jacques Monod, *Le hasard et la necessité, essai sur la philosophie naturelle de la biologie moderne* (Paris: Seuil, 1970), p. 142. English trans.: *Chance and Necessity: An Essay on the Natural Philosophy of Modern Biology* (New York: Knopf, 1971), p. 127.

3. Ibid., French edition, p. 141; English trans., pp. 125–26.

4. Such parallels have nevertheless been suggested by Britten and Davidson in their theory of genic regulation (1969).

Index

About the Author

A prolific writer on philosophy and biology as well as the father of the developmental psychology he calls genetic epistemology, Jean Piaget has had as his main area of concern the genesis of abstract concepts (classes, relations, numbers) and physical concepts (space, speed, chance, time) in the developing child. His theories have been widely applied to education.

Among Piaget's more general works include *Insights and Illusions of Philosophy; Structuralism;* and the study most closely connected to this book, *Biology and Knowledge.*